CREATIVITY

ALSO BY OSHO

The Book of Secrets

Osho Zen Tarot

Meditation: The First and Last Freedom

Courage

Maturity

Osho Transformation Tarot

AUDIO

The Book of Secrets

Osho Meditations on Zen

Osho Meditations on Tao

Osho Meditations on Yoga

Osho Meditations on Buddhism

Osho Meditations on Sufism

Osho Meditations on Tantra

Monica

CREATIVITY

unleashing the
Forces Within

osho

·

*insights for a
new way of living*

St. Martin's Griffin ❦ New York

CREATIVITY: UNLEASHING THE FORCES WITHIN. Copyright © 1999
by Osho International Foundation. All rights reserved. Printed in the
United States of America. No part of this book may be used or
reproduced in any manner whatsoever without written permission
except in the case of brief quotations embodied in critical articles or
reviews. For information address St. Martin's Press, 175 Fifth Avenue,
New York, N.Y. 10010.

Book design by Claire Vaccaro

Library of Congress Cataloging-in-Publication Data

Osho, 1931–1990.
    Creativity : unleashing the forces within / Osho. — 1st St.
Martin's Griffin ed.
        p.   cm. — (Insights for a new way of living)
    ISBN 0-312-20519-8
    1. Spiritual life.   2. Creative ability—Religious aspects.
I. Title.   II. Series: Osho, 1931–1990. Insights for a new way of
living.
BP605.R34C74   1999
299'.93—dc21   99-32895
                                                                        CIP

3   5   7   9   10   8   6   4   2

Contents

FOREWORD   *ix*
The Fragrance of Freedom

PREPARING THE CANVAS   *1*
   The Three C's   *1*
   Relax in Action   *3*
   Act in Harmony with Nature   *31*

FIVE OBSTACLES   *39*
   1. Self-Consciousness   *39*
   2. Perfectionism   *71*
   3. Intellect   *77*
   4. Belief   *87*
   5. The Fame Game   *103*

FOUR KEYS   *108*
   1. Become a Child Again   *108*
   2. Be Ready to Learn   *118*
   3. Find Nirvana in the Ordinary   *121*
   4. Be a Dreamer   *130*

FOUR QUESTIONS   *136*
   1. Memory and Imagination   *136*
   2. Postpartum Depression   *157*

Contents

3. Creativity and Crossbreeding   163

4. The Art of Money   ?   (171)

CREATION   181

The Ultimate Creativity, the Meaning of Your Life

ABOUT THE AUTHOR   192

MEDITATION RESORT   193

Osho Commune International

Foreword

❧

The Fragrance of Freedom

Creativity is the greatest rebellion in existence. If you want to create you have to get rid of all conditionings; otherwise your creativity will be nothing but copying, it will be just a carbon copy. You can be creative only if you are an individual, you cannot create as a part of the mob psychology. The mob psychology is uncreative; it lives a dragging life, it knows no dance, no song, no joy; it is mechanical.

The creator cannot follow the well-trodden path. He has to search out his own way, he has to inquire in the jungles of life. He has to go alone; he has to be a dropout from the mob mind, from the collective psychology. The collective mind is the lowest mind in the world—even so-called idiots are superior to the collective idiocy. But the collectivity has its own bribes: it respects people, honors people if they go on insisting that the way of the collective mind is the only right way.

It was out of sheer necessity that in the past, creators of all kinds—the painters, the dancers, the musicians, the poets, the sculptors—had to renounce respectability. They had to live a kind of bohemian life, the life of a vagabond; that was the only possibility for them to be creative. This need not be so in the future. If you understand me, if you feel what I am saying has truth in it, then in the future everybody should live individually and there will be no need for a bohemian life. The bohemian life is the by-product of a

> The creator cannot follow the well-trodden path. He has to go alone, he has to be a dropout from the mob mind, from the collective psychology.

fixed, orthodox, conventional, respectable life.

My effort is to destroy the collective mind and to make each individual free to be himself or herself. Then there is no problem; then you can live as you want to live. In fact, humanity will really be born only the day the individual is respected in his rebellion. Humanity has still not been born; it is still in the womb. What you see as humanity is only a very hocus-pocus phenomenon. Unless we give individual freedom to each person, absolute freedom to each person to be himself, to exist in his own way . . . And, of course, he has not to interfere with anybody—that is part of freedom. Nobody should interfere with anybody.

But in the past everybody has been poking his nose into everybody else's affairs—even into things that are absolutely private, which have nothing to do with the society. For example, you fall in love with a woman, what has that got to do with the society? It is purely a personal phenomenon, it is not of the marketplace. If two persons are agreeing to commune in love the society should not come into it. But the society comes into it with all its paraphernalia, in direct ways, in indirect ways. The policeman will stand between the lovers, the magistrate will stand between the lovers. And if that is not enough then the societies have created a super-policeman, God, who will take care of you.

The idea of God is that of a Peeping Tom who does not even

allow you privacy in your bathroom, who goes on looking through the keyhole, watching what you are doing. This is ugly! All the religions of the world say God continuously watches you—this is ugly, what kind of God is this? Has he got no other business but to watch everybody, follow everybody? Seems to be the ultimate detective!

Humanity needs a new soil—the soil of freedom. Bohemianism was a reaction, a necessary reaction, but if my vision succeeds then there will be no bohemianism because there will be no so-called collective mind trying to dominate people. Then everybody will be at ease with himself. Of course, you have not to interfere with anybody—but as far as your life is concerned you have to live it on your own terms.

Then only is there creativity. Creativity is the fragrance of individual freedom.

A creative person is one who has insight, who can see things nobody else has ever seen before, who hears things that nobody has heard before— then there is creativity.

PREPARING THE CANVAS

❧

Once pathology disappears, everybody becomes a creator. Let it be understood as deeply as possible: only ill people are destructive. The people who are healthy are creative. Creativity is a fragrance of real health. When a person is really healthy and whole, creativity comes naturally to him, the urge to create arises.

THE THREE C'S

Humanity has come now to a crossroads. We have lived the one-dimensional man, we have exhausted it. We need now a more enriched human being, three-dimensional. I call them three *C*'s, just like three R's—the first C is consciousness, the second C is compassion, the third C is creativity.

Consciousness is being, compassion is feeling, creativity is action. My vision of the new human being has to be all the three simultaneously. I am giving you the greatest challenge ever given, the hardest task to be fulfilled. You have to be as meditative as a Buddha, as loving as a Krishna, as creative as Michelangelo, Leonardo da Vinci. You have to be all together, simultaneously. Only then your totality will be fulfilled; otherwise something will remain missing in you. And that which is missing in you will keep you lopsided, unfulfilled. You can attain a very high peak if you are one-dimensional, but you will be only a peak. I would like you to become the whole range of the Himalayas, not just a peak but peaks upon peaks.

The one-dimensional man has failed. It has not been able to create a beautiful earth, it has not been able to create paradise on the earth. It has failed, utterly failed! It created a few beautiful people but it could not transform the whole humanity, it could not raise the consciousness of the whole humanity. Only a few individuals here and there became enlightened. That is not going to help anymore. We need more enlightened people, and enlightened in a three-dimensional way.

> You can attain a very high peak if you are one-dimensional, but you will be only a peak. I would like you to become the whole range of the Himalayas, not just a peak but peaks upon peaks.

That is my definition of the new man.

Buddha was not a poet—but the new humanity, the people who will become buddhas now, are going to be poets. When I say "poets" I don't mean that you have to write poetry—you have to be poetic. Your life has to be poetic, your approach has to be poetic.

Logic is dry, poetry is alive. Logic cannot dance; it is impossible for logic to dance. To see logic dancing will be like Mahatma Gandhi dancing! It will look very ridiculous. Poetry can dance; poetry is a dance of your heart. Logic cannot love—it can talk about love but it cannot love; love seems to be illogical. Only poetry can love, only poetry can take the jump into the paradox of love.

Logic is cold, very cold; it is good as far as mathematics is concerned but it is not good as far as humanity is concerned. If humanity becomes too logical, then humanity disappears; then there are only numbers, not human beings—replaceable numbers.

Poetry, love, and feeling give you a depth, a warmth. You become more melted, you lose your coldness. You become more human. Buddha is superhuman, about that there is no doubt, but he loses the human dimension. He is unearthly. He has a beauty of being unearthly, but he does not have the beauty that Zorba the Greek has. Zorba is so earthly. I would like you to be both together—Zorba the Buddha. One has to be meditative but not against feeling. One has to be meditative but full of feeling, overflowing with love. And one has to be creative. If your love is only a feeling and it is not translated into action, it won't affect the larger humanity. You have to make it a reality, you have to materialize it.

These are your three dimensions: being, feeling, action. Action contains creativity, all kinds of creativity—music, poetry, painting, sculpture, architecture, science, technology. Feeling contains all that is aesthetic—love, beauty. And being contains meditation, awareness, consciousness.

RELAX IN ACTION

First, the nature of activity and the hidden currents in it have to be understood; otherwise no relaxation is possible. Even if you want to relax, it will be impossible if you have not observed, watched, realized, the nature of your activity, because activity is not a simple phenomenon. Many people would like to relax, but they cannot. Relaxation is like a flowering, you cannot force it. You have to understand the whole phenomenon—why you are so active, why so much occupation with activity, why you are obsessed with it.

Remember two words: one is *action,* another is *activity.* Action is not activity; activity is not action. Their natures are diametrically opposite. Action is when the situation demands it and you act, you respond. Activity is when the situation doesn't matter, it is not a response; you are so restless within that the situation is just an excuse to be active.

Action comes out of a silent mind—it is the most beautiful thing in the world. Activity comes out of a restless mind—it is the ugliest. Action is when it has relevance; activity is irrelevant. Action is moment to moment, spontaneous; activity is loaded with the past. It is not a response to the present moment, rather, it is pouring your restlessness, which you have been carrying from the past, into the present. Action is creative. Activity is very destructive—it destroys you, it destroys others.

> Buddha has the beauty of being unearthly, but he does not have the beauty that Zorba the Greek has. Zorba is so earthly. I would like you to be both together—Zorba the Buddha. One has to be meditative but not against feeling.

Try to see the delicate distinction. For example, you are hungry, then you eat—this is action. But you are not hungry, you don't feel any hunger at all, and still you go on eating—this is activity.

This eating is a kind of violence: you destroy food, you crush your teeth together and destroy food; it gives you a little release of your inner restlessness. You are eating not because of hunger, you are simply eating because of an inner need, an urge to be violent.

In the animal world violence is associated with the mouth and hands, the fingernails and the teeth; these two are the violent things in the animal kingdom. While you are eating, both are joined together; with your hand you take the food, and with your mouth you eat it—violence is released. But if there is no hunger it is not an *action*, it is a disease. This activity is an obsession. Of course you cannot go on eating like this because then you will burst, so people have invented tricks: they will chew tobacco or gum, they will smoke cigarettes. These are false foods, without any nutritious value in them, but they work well as far as violence is concerned.

Relaxation is like a flowering, you cannot force it. You have to understand the whole phenomenon—why you are so active, why so much occupation with activity, why you are obsessed with it.

A man sitting and chewing gum, what is he doing? He is killing somebody. In the mind, if he becomes aware, he may have a fantasy of murdering, killing—and he is chewing gum, a very innocent activity in itself. You are not harming anybody—but very dangerous for you, because you seem to be completely unconscious of what you are doing. A man smoking, what is he doing? Very innocent in a way, just taking the smoke in and bringing it out, inhaling and exhaling—a sort of ill *pranayama*, and a sort of secular transcendental meditation. He is creating a mandala: he takes smoke in, brings it out, takes it in, brings it out—a mandala is created, a circle. Through smoking he is doing a sort of chanting, a rhythmic chanting. It soothes; his inner restlessness is relieved a little.

If you are talking to a person, always remember—it is almost hundred percent accurate—if the person starts reaching for his cigarette, it means he is bored, you should leave him now. He would have wanted to throw you out; that cannot be done, that will be too impolite. He is finding his cigarette; he is saying, "Now, finished! I am fed up." In the animal kingdom he would have jumped on you, but he cannot—he is a human being, civilized. He jumps on the cigarette, he starts smoking. Now he is not worried about you, now he is enclosed in his own chanting of the smoke. It soothes.

But this activity shows that you are obsessed. You cannot remain yourself; you cannot remain silent, you cannot remain inactive. Through activity you go on throwing out your madness, insanity.

Action is beautiful, action comes as a spontaneous response. Life needs response, every moment you have to act, but the activity comes through the present moment. You are hungry and you seek food, you are thirsty and you go to the well. You are feeling sleepy and you go to sleep. It is out of the total situation that you act. Action is spontaneous and total.

Activity is never spontaneous, it comes from the past. You may have been accumulating it for many years, and then it explodes into the present—it is not relevant. But mind is cunning; the mind will always find rationalizations for the activity. The mind will always try to prove that this is not activity, this is action; it was needed. Suddenly you flare up in anger. Everybody else becomes aware that it was not needed, the situation never demanded it, it was simply irrelevant—only you cannot see. Everybody feels, "What are you doing? There was no need for it. Why are you so angry?" But you will find rationalizations, you will rationalize that it was needed.

These rationalizations help you to remain unconscious about your madness. These are the things that George Gurdjieff used to call "buffers." You create buffers of rationalization around you so you don't come to realize what is the situation. Buffers are used in trains, between two compartments; buffers are used so that if there is a sudden stopping there will not be too much shock to the passengers. The buffers will absorb the shock. Your activity is continuously irrelevant, but the buffers of rationalizations don't allow you to see the situation. The buffers blind you, and this type of activity continues.

If this activity is there, you cannot relax. How can you relax?—because it is an obsessive need, you want to do something, whatsoever it is. There are fools all over the world who go on saying, "Do something rather than nothing." And there are perfect fools who have created a proverb all over the world, "An empty mind is a devil's workshop." It is not! An empty mind is God's workshop. An empty mind is the most beautiful thing in the world, the purest. How can an empty mind be a workshop for the devil? The devil cannot enter into an empty mind, impossible! The devil can enter only into a mind which is obsessed with activity—then the devil can take charge of you, he can show you ways and means and methods to be more active. The devil never says, "Relax!" He says, "Why are you wasting your time? Do something, man—move! Life is passing by, do something!" And all the great teachers, teachers who have awakened to the truth of life, have come to realize that an empty mind gives space to the divine to enter in you.

Activity can be used by the devil, not an empty mind. How can the devil use an empty mind? He will not dare to come near because emptiness will simply kill him. But if you are filled with a deep urge, a mad urge to be active, then the devil will take charge. Then he will guide you—then he is the only guide.

I would like to tell you that this proverb is absolutely wrong. The devil himself must have suggested it.

This obsession to be active has to be watched. And you have to watch it in your own life, because whatsoever I say will not be of much meaning unless you see it in yourself that your activity is irrelevant, it is not needed. Why are you doing it?

Traveling, I have seen people continuously doing the same thing again and again. For twenty-four hours I am with a passenger in the train. He will read the same newspaper again, again, not finding what else to do. Enclosed in a railway compartment there is not much possibility to be active, so he will read the same newspaper again and again. And I am watching . . . what is this man doing?

> There are perfect fools who have created a proverb all over the world that "An empty mind is a devil's workshop." It is not! An empty mind is God's workshop.

A newspaper is not a Gita or a Bible. You can read the Gita many times because each time you come to it a new significance is revealed. But a newspaper is not a Gita; it is finished once you have seen it! It was not even worth reading once, and people go on reading it. Again and again, they will start again. What is the problem? Is it a need? No—they are obsessed; they cannot remain silent, inactive.

That is impossible for them, that looks like death. They have to be active.

Traveling for many years gave me many opportunities to watch people without their knowing, because sometimes only one person was with me in the compartment. And he would make all sorts of efforts to bring me to talk to him and I would say only yes or no; then he would drop the idea. Then I would simply watch—a beautiful experiment, and without any expense! I would watch him: he would open the suitcase—and I would see that he was not doing anything—then he would look in it, close it. Then he would open the window, and then would close it. Then again he would go to the newspaper, then he would smoke, then again open the suitcase, rearrange it, go and open the window, look out. What is he doing? And why? An inner urge, something is trembling within him, a feverish state of mind. He has to do something, otherwise he will be lost. He must have been an active man in life; now there is a moment to relax—he cannot relax, the old habit persists.

It is said that Aurangzeb, a Moghul emperor, imprisoned his father in his old age. Aurangzeb's father, Shah Jehan, built the Taj Mahal. The son imprisoned him, dethroned him.

> When you want to climb to the highest peak of the mountains, it is arduous. And when you have reached the peak and you lie down, whispering with the clouds, looking at the sky, the joy that fills your heart—that joy always comes whenever you reach any peak of creativity.

It is said, and it is written in the autobiography of Aurangzeb, that after a few days Shah Jehan was not worried about imprisonment because every luxury was provided. It was a palace, and Shah Jehan was living as he was living before. It was not like a prison; absolutely everything that he needed was there. Only one thing was missing and that was activity—he couldn't do anything. So he asked his son Aurangzeb, "It is okay, you have provided everything for me and everything is beautiful. Just one thing I will be grateful forever and ever if you can do and that is, send thirty boys. I would like to teach them."

Aurangzeb could not believe it: "Why would my father like to teach thirty boys?" He had never shown any inclination to be a teacher, was never interested in any type of education, what has happened to him? But he fulfilled the desire. Thirty boys were sent to Shah Jehan, and everything was okay—he became again the emperor, thirty small boys. You go into a primary school, the teacher is almost the emperor. You can order them to sit and they will have to sit; you can order them to stand and they will have to stand. And he created in that room with thirty boys the whole situation of his court—just old habit and the old drug addiction to ordering people.

Psychologists suspect that teachers are in fact politicians. Of course, not self-confident enough to go into politics—they move to the schools and there they become presidents, prime ministers, emperors. Small children—and they order them and they force them. Psychologists also suspect that teachers have an inclination toward being sadistic, they would like to torture. And you cannot find a better place than a primary school. You can torture innocent children—and you can torture them for their own sake, for their own good. Go and watch! I have been in primary schools, and I have been watching teachers. Psychologists suspect—I am *certain* they are torturers! And you cannot find more innocent victims, unarmed completely, they cannot even resist. They are so weak and helpless—and a teacher stands like an emperor.

Aurangzeb writes in his autobiography: "My father, just because of old habits, still wants to pretend that he is the emperor. So let him pretend and let him fool himself, there is nothing wrong. Send him thirty boys or three hundred, whatsoever he wants. Let him run a small school and be happy."

Activity is when the action has no relevance. Watch in yourself and see: ninety percent of your energy is wasted in activity. And because of this, when the moment for action comes you don't have any energy. A relaxed person is simply non-obsessive, and the energy starts accumulating within him. He conserves his energy, it is conserved automatically, and then when the moment for action comes his total being flows into it. That's why action is total. Activity is always halfhearted, because how can you befool yourself absolutely? Even you know it is useless. Even you are aware that you are doing it for certain feverish reasons within, which are not even clear to you, very vague.

You can change activities, but unless activities are transformed into actions that won't help. People come to me and they say, "I would like to stop smoking." I say, "Why? This is such a beautiful TM, continue." And if you stop it, you will start some-

> A relaxed person is simply non-obsessive, and the energy starts accumulating within him. He conserves his energy, and then when the moment for action comes his total being flows into it.

11

thing else—because the disease doesn't change by changing the symptoms. Then you will bite your nails, then you will chew gum—and there are even more dangerous things. These are innocent, because if you are chewing gum you are chewing gum yourself. You may be a fool but you are not a violent man, you are not destructive to anybody else. If you stop chewing gum, smoking, then what will you do? Your mouth needs activity, it is violent. Then you will talk. Then you will talk continuously—yakety-yakety-yak—and that is more dangerous!

Mulla Nasruddin's wife came just the other day. She rarely comes to see me, but when she comes I immediately understand there must be some crisis. So I asked, "What is the matter?" Thirty minutes she took, and thousands of words, to tell me, "Mulla Nasruddin talks in his sleep, so you suggest something—what should be done? He talks too much and it is difficult to sleep in the same room. And he shouts and says nasty things."

So I said, "Nothing is to be done. You simply give him a chance to talk while you are both awake."

People go on talking, they don't give any chance to anybody else. Talking is the same as smoking. If you talk twenty-four hours . . . and you do talk! While you are awake, you talk; then your body is tired, you fall into sleep, but the talk continues. Twenty-four hours, round the clock, you go on talking and talking and talking. This is like smoking, because the phenomenon is the same: the mouth needs movement. And the mouth is the basic activity because that is the first activity you started in your life.

The child is born, he starts sucking the mother's breast—that is the first activity and the basic activity. Smoking is just like sucking the breast: warm milk flows in . . . in smoking, warm smoke flows in, and the cigarette in your lips feels just like the breast of the mother, the nipple. If you are not allowed to smoke, chew gum and this and that, then you will talk. And that is more dangerous because you are throwing your garbage on other people's minds.

Can you remain silent for a long time? Psychologists say that if you remain silent for three weeks you will start talking to yourself. Then you will be divided into two: you will talk and you will listen also. And if you try to remain silent for three months, you will be completely ready for the madhouse, because then you will not bother whether somebody is there or not. You will talk, and not only talk, you will answer also—now you are complete, now you don't depend on anybody. This is what a lunatic is.

A lunatic is a person whose whole world is confined in himself. He is the talker and he is the listener, he is the actor and he is the spectator—he is all, his whole world is confined in himself. He has divided himself in many parts, and everything has become fragmentary. That's why people are afraid of silence—they know they may crack up. And if you are afraid of silence that means you have an obsessive, feverish, diseased mind inside, which is continuously asking to be active.

Activity is your escape from yourself. In action *you are*; in activity you have escaped from yourself—it is a drug. In activity you forget yourself, and when you forget yourself there are no worries, no anguish, no anxiety. That's why you need to be continuously active, doing something or other, but never in a state when non-doing flowers in you and blooms.

Action is good. Activity is ill. Find the distinction within yourself: what is activity and what is action? That is the first step. The second step is to be more involved in action so that the energy moves into action; and whenever there is activity to be more watchful about it, more alert. If you are aware, activity ceases. Energy is preserved, and the same energy becomes action.

Action is immediate. It is nothing ready-made, it is not prefabricated. It doesn't give you any chance to make a preparation, to go through a rehearsal. Action is always new and fresh like the dewdrops in the morning. And a person who is a person of action is also always fresh and young. The body may become old but his freshness continues; the body may die but his youth continues. The body may disappear but he remains—because God loves freshness. God is always for the new and the fresh.

Drop more and more activity. But how can you drop it? You can make dropping itself an obsession. This is what has happened to your monks in the monasteries: dropping activity has become their obsession. They are continuously doing something to drop it—prayer, meditation, yoga, this and that. Now, that is also activity. You cannot drop it in that way, it will come from the back door.

Be aware. Feel the difference between action and activity. And when activity takes hold of you—in fact that should be called a possession—when the activity possesses you, like a ghost—and activity is a ghost, it comes from the past, it is dead—when activity possesses you and you become feverish, then become more aware. That's all you can do. Watch it. Even if you have to do it, do it with full awareness. Smoke, but smoke very slowly, with full awareness so that you can see what you are doing.

If you can watch smoking, suddenly some day the cigarette will fall from your fingers because the whole absurdity of it will be revealed to you. It is stupid; it is simply stupid, idiotic. When you realize that, it simply falls. You cannot throw it because throwing is an activity. That's why I say it simply falls, just like a dead leaf from the tree . . . falling, just like that it falls. If you have thrown it you will pick it up again in some other way, in some other form.

Let things drop, don't drop them. Let activity disappear, don't force it to disappear—because the very effort to force it to disappear is again activity in another form. Watch, be alert, conscious, and you will come to a miraculous phenomenon: when something drops by itself, on its own accord, it leaves no trace on you. If you force it then a trace is left, then a scar is left. Then you will always brag that you smoked for thirty years and then you dropped it. Now this bragging is the same. Talking about it, you are doing the same thing—not smoking, but talking too much about the fact that you have dropped smoking. Your lips are again in activity, your mouth is functioning, your violence is there.

> It is not a question of what you do, it is a question of how you do it. And ultimately it is a question whether you do it or you allow it to happen.

If a man really understands, things drop—and then you cannot take the credit that "I have dropped it." It dropped itself! You have not dropped it. The ego is not strengthened through it. And then more and more actions will become possible.

And whenever you have an opportunity to act totally, don't miss it, don't waver—act. Act more, and let activities drop of their own accord. A transformation will come to you by and by. It takes time, it needs seasoning, but there is no hurry.

Listen to these words of Tilopa*:

Do nought with the body but relax; shut firm the mouth
and silent remain; empty your mind and think of nought.

"Do nought with the body but relax. . . ." Now you can understand what relaxation means. It means no urge to activity in you.
Relaxation doesn't mean lying down like a dead man—and you
cannot lie down like a dead man, you can only pretend. How can
you lie down like a dead man? You are alive, you can only pretend.
Relaxation comes to you when there is no urge to activity; the
energy is at home, not moving anywhere. If a certain situation arises
you will act, that's all, but you are not finding some excuse to act.
You are at ease with yourself. Relaxation is to be at home.

I was reading one book a few years ago. The title of the book
is *You Must Relax*. This is simply ab-
surd, because the "must" is against
relaxation—but such books can sell
only in America. "Must" means activity, it is an obsession. Whenever
there is a "must," an obsession is hidden behind it. There are actions in
life, but there is no "must," otherwise the "must" will create madness.
"You must relax"—now relaxation
has become the obsession. You have
to do this posture and that, and lie
down, and suggest to your body from

> ⁊
>
> Relaxation comes only
> when there is no
> "must" in your life.
> Relaxation is not only
> of the body, it is not
> only of the mind, it
> is of your total being.

*An eleventh-century mystic who carried Buddha's teachings from India to Tibet the toes to the head; tell the toes, "Relax!" and then go upward. . . .

Why "must"? Relaxation comes only when there is no "must" in your life. Relaxation is not only of the body, it is not only of the mind, it is of your total being.

You are too much in activity, of course tired, dissipated, dried up, frozen. The life-energy doesn't move. There are only blocks and blocks and blocks. And whenever you do something, you do it in a state of madness. Of course the need to relax arises! That's why so many books are written every month about relaxation. And I have never seen a person who has become relaxed through reading a book about relaxation—he has become more hectic, because now his whole life of activity remains untouched, his obsession is there to be active, the disease is there, and he pretends to be in a relaxed state. So he lies down, all turmoil within, a volcano ready to erupt, and he is relaxing, following the instructions from a book: "how to relax."

There is no book that can help you to relax—unless you read your own inner being, and then relaxation is not a "must." Relaxation is an absence, absence of activity. Not of *action*—there is no need to move to the Himalayas—a few people have done that; to

> The mind should remain alive and creative, and yet should be capable of moving into silence whenever it wants to. That's mastery. When you want to think, you can think; when you don't want to think, you can go into non-thinking. A real master is one who can do both.

relax, they move to the Himalayas. What is the need to move to the Himalayas? Action is not to be dropped, because if you drop action, you drop life. Then you will be dead, not relaxed. In the Himalayas you will find sages who are dead, not relaxed. They have escaped from life, from action.

This is the subtle point to be understood: activity has to go, but not action. Dropping both is easy—you can drop both and escape to the Himalayas, that's easy. Or the other thing is easy: you can continue in the activities and force yourself every morning or every evening, for a few minutes, to relax. You don't understand the complexity of the human mind, the mechanism of it. Relaxation is a state. You cannot force it. You simply drop the negativities, the hindrances, and it comes, it bubbles up by itself.

What do you do when you go to sleep in the night? Do you do something? If you do, you will be an insomniac, you will move into insomnia. What do you do? You simply lie down and go into sleep. There is no "doing" to it. If you "do," it will be impossible to sleep. In fact, to go into sleep all that is needed is, the continuity in the mind of the activities of the day has to discontinue. That's all! When the

> I have never seen a person who has become relaxed through reading a book about relaxation—he has become more hectic, because now his whole life of activity remains untouched, his obsession is there to be active, the disease is there, and he pretends to be in a relaxed state.

activity is not there in the mind, the mind relaxes and goes into sleep. If you do something to go into sleep, you will be at a loss, then sleep will be impossible.

Doing is not needed at all. Says Tilopa, "Do nought with the body but relax." Don't do anything! No yoga posture is needed, no distortions and contortions of the body are needed. "Do nought!"—only absence of activity is needed. And how will it come? It will come by understanding. Understanding is the only discipline. Understand your activities and suddenly, in the middle of the activity, if you become aware, it will stop. If you become aware why you are doing it, it will stop. And that stopping is what Tilopa means: "Do nought with the body but relax."

What is relaxation? It is a state of affairs where your energy is not moving anywhere—not to the future, not to the past, it is simply there with you. In the silent pool of your own energy, in the warmth of it, you are enveloped. This moment is all. There is no other moment, time stops—then there is relaxation. If time is there, there is no relaxation. Simply the clock stops; there is no time; this moment is all. You don't ask for anything else, you simply enjoy it. Ordinary things can be enjoyed because they are beautiful. In fact, nothing is ordinary—then everything is extraordinary.

People come to me and ask, "Do you believe in God?" I say, "Yes, because everything is so extraordinary, how can it be without

> Relaxation is a state. You cannot force it. You simply drop the negativities, the hindrances, and it comes, it bubbles up by itself.

a deep consciousness in it?" Just small things . . . Walking on the lawn when the dewdrops have not evaporated yet, and just feeling totally there—the texture, the touch of the lawn, the coolness of the dewdrops, the morning wind, the sun rising. What more do you need to be happy? What more is possible to be happy? Just lying down in the night on the cool sheet on your bed, feeling the texture; feeling that the sheet is getting warmer and warmer, and you are shrouded in darkness, the silence of the night . . . With closed eyes you simply feel yourself. What more do you need? It is too much—a deep gratitude arises. This is relaxation.

Relaxation means this moment is more than enough, more than can be asked and expected. Nothing to ask, more than enough, more than you can desire—then the energy never moves anywhere, it becomes a placid pool. In your own energy, you dissolve. This moment is relaxation.

Relaxation is neither of the body nor of the mind, relaxation is of the total. That's why the buddhas go on saying, "Become desireless," because they know that if there is desire you cannot relax. They go on saying, "Bury the dead," because if you are too much concerned with the past you cannot relax. They go

> Understanding is the only discipline. Understand your activities and suddenly, in the middle of the activity, if you become aware, it will stop. If you become aware why you are doing it, it will stop. And that stopping is what Tilopa means: "Do nought with the body but relax."

on saying, "Enjoy this very moment." Jesus says, "Look at the lilies. Consider the lilies in the field—they toil not and they are more beautiful, their splendor is greater than King Solomon. They are arrayed in more beautiful aroma than King Solomon ever was. Look, consider the lilies!"

What is he saying? He is saying, relax! You need not toil for it—in fact, everything is provided. Jesus says, "If he looks after the birds of air, animals, wild animals, trees and plants, then why are you worried? Will he not look after you?" This is relaxation. Why are you so much worried about the future? Consider the lilies, watch the lilies, and become like lilies—and then relax. Relaxation is not a posture; relaxation is a total transformation of your energy.

Energy can have two dimensions. One is motivated, going somewhere, a goal somewhere—this moment is only a means, and the goal is somewhere else to be achieved. This is one dimension of your energy: this is the dimension of activity, goal-oriented, then everything is a means. Somehow it has to be done and you have to reach to the goal, then you will relax. But for this type of energy the goal is never reached, because this type of energy goes on changing every present moment into a means for something else, into the future. The goal always remains on the horizon. You go on running, but the distance remains the same.

No, there is another dimension

> Energy is good, energy is delight, energy is divine. Once energy is released one can become creative. It brings intelligence, creativity, sensitivity, it brings all that is beautiful.

> ❧
>
> Energy needs work,
> otherwise the energy
> will become
> restlessness. Energy
> needs expression,
> energy needs to be
> creative. Otherwise
> the same energy,
> coiled up within you,
> will become diseased,
> an illness.

of energy: that dimension is unmotivated celebration. The goal is here, now, the goal is not somewhere else. In fact, *you are* the goal. In fact, there is no other fulfillment than of this moment—consider the lilies. When *you are* the goal and when the goal is not in the future—when there is nothing to be achieved, rather, you have just to celebrate it, you have already achieved it, it is there—this is relaxation, unmotivated energy.

So, to me, there are two types of persons: the goal seekers and the celebrators. The goal-oriented are the mad ones. They are going, by and by, crazy—and they are creating their own craziness. And then the craziness has its own momentum; by and by they move deeper into it—then they are completely lost. The other type of person is not a goal seeker; he is not a seeker at all, he is a celebrator. me

Be the celebrators, celebrate! Already there is too much—the flowers have bloomed, the birds are singing, the sun is there in the sky—celebrate it! You are breathing and you are alive and you have consciousness, celebrate it! Then suddenly you relax; then there is no tension, then there is no anguish. The whole energy that becomes anguish becomes gratitude. Your whole heart goes on beating with a deep thankfulness—that is prayer. That's all prayer is about, a heart beating with a deep thankfulness.

Do nought with the body but relax. No need to do anything for it. Just understand the movement of the energy, the unmotivated movement of the energy. It flows, but not toward a goal, it flows as a celebration. It moves, not toward a goal, it moves because of its own overflowing energy.

A child is dancing and jumping and running around. Ask him, "Where are you going?" He is not going anywhere—you will look foolish to him. Children always think adults are foolish. What a nonsense question, "Where are you going?" Is there any need to go anywhere? A child simply cannot answer your question because it is irrelevant. He is not going anywhere. He will simply shrug his shoulders. He will say, "Nowhere." Then the goal-oriented mind asks, "Then why are you running?"—because to us an activity is relevant only when it leads somewhere.

And I tell you, there is nowhere to go. Here is all. The whole existence culminates in this moment, it converges into this moment. The whole existence is pouring already into this moment. All that is, is pouring into this moment—it is here, now. A child is simply enjoying the energy. He has so much! He is running not because he has to reach somewhere but because he has too much; he has to run.

Act unmotivated, just an overflow of your energy. Share but don't trade, don't make bargains. Give because you have, don't give to take back—because then you will be in misery. All traders go to hell. If you want to find the greatest traders and bargainers go to hell, there you will find them. Heaven is not for traders, heaven is for celebrators.

In Christian theology, again and again, for centuries it has been asked, "What do angels do in heaven?" This is a relevant question for people who are goal oriented: "What do angels do in heaven?" Nothing seems to be done, nothing is there to do. Somebody asked

Meister Eckhart, "What do angels do in heaven?" He said, "What type of a fool are you? Heaven is a place to celebrate. They don't do anything. They simply celebrate—the glory of it, the magnificence of it, the poetry of it, the blooming of it, they celebrate. They sing and they dance and they celebrate." But I don't think that man was satisfied by Meister Eckhart's answer, because to us an activity is meaningful only if it leads somewhere, if there is a goal.

> ॐ
>
> Act unmotivated, just an overflow of your energy. Share but don't trade, don't make bargains. Give because you have, don't give to take back—because then you will be in misery. All traders go to hell.

Remember, activity is goal oriented, action is not. Action is overflowing of energy. Action is in this moment, a response, unprepared, unrehearsed. Just the whole existence meets you, confronts you, and a response comes. The birds are singing and you start singing—it is not an activity. Suddenly it happens. Suddenly you find it is happening, that you have started humming—this is action.

And if you become more and more involved in action, and less and less occupied in activity, your life will change and it will become a deep relaxation. Then you "do" but you remain relaxed.

A buddha is never tired. Why?—because he is not a doer. Whatsoever he has, he gives, he overflows.

Do nought with the body but relax; shut firm the mouth and silent remain. The mouth is really very significant, because that is where the first activity landed; your lips started the first activity. Surrounding the area of the mouth is the beginning of all activity—you breathed in, you cried, you started groping for the mother's breast. And your mouth remains always in a frantic activity. That's why Tilopa suggests, "Understand activity, understand action, relax, and . . . *shut firm the mouth*."

Whenever you sit down to meditate, whenever you want to be silent, the first thing is to shut the mouth completely. If you shut the mouth completely, your tongue will touch the roof of your mouth; the lips will be completely closed and the tongue will touch the roof. Shut it completely—but that can be done only if you have followed whatsoever I have been saying to you, not before it. You can do it, shutting the mouth is not a very big effort. You can sit like a statue with a completely shut mouth, but that will not stop activity. Deep inside the thinking will continue, and if thinking continues you can feel subtle vibrations in the lips. Others may not be able to observe it because they are very subtle, but if you are thinking then your lips quiver a little—a very subtle quivering.

> If you become more and more involved in action, and less and less occupied in activity, your life will change and it will become a deep relaxation. Then you "do" but you remain relaxed. A Buddha is never tired. Why?—because he is not a doer. Whatsoever he has, he gives, he overflows.

When you really relax, that quivering stops. You are not talking, you are not making any activity inside you. *Shut firm the mouth and silent remain*—and then don't think.

What will you do? Thoughts are coming and going. Let them come and go, that's not a problem. You don't get involved; you remain aloof, detached. You simply watch them coming and going, they are not your concern. Shut the mouth and remain silent. By and by, thoughts will cease automatically—they need your cooperation to be there. If you cooperate, they will be there; if you fight, then too they will be there, because both are cooperations—one for, the other against. Both are sorts of activity. You simply watch.

But shutting of the mouth is very helpful.

So first, as I have been observing many people, I will suggest to you that first you yawn. Open your mouth as wide as possible, tense your mouth as wide as possible, yawn completely so it even starts hurting. Two or three times do this. This will help the mouth to remain shut for a longer time. And then for two or three minutes talk loudly, gibberish, nonsense. Anything that comes to the mind, say it loudly and enjoy it. Then shut the mouth.

It is easier to move from the opposite end. If you want to relax your hand, it is better to first make it as tense as possible—clench the fist and let it be as tense as possible. Do just the opposite and then relax. And then you will attain a deeper relaxation of the nervous system. Make gestures, faces, movements of the face, distortions, yawn, talk two or three minutes of nonsense—and then shut the mouth. And this tension will give you a deeper possibility to relax the lips and mouth. Shut the mouth and then just be a watcher. Soon a silence will descend on you.

There are two types of silences. One is a silence that you can force upon yourself. That is not a very graceful thing. It is a kind of violence, it is a sort of rape on the mind; it is aggressive. Then there is another sort of silence that descends on you like night descends. It comes upon you, it envelops you. You simply create the possibility for it, the receptivity, and it comes. Shut the mouth, watch. Don't try to be silent. If you try, you can force a few seconds of silence but they will not be of any value—inside you will go on boiling. So don't try to be silent. You simply create the situation, the soil, plant the seed and wait.

Empty your mind and think of nought.

What will you do to empty the mind? Thoughts are coming, you watch. And watching has to be done with a precaution: the watching must be passive, not active. These are subtle mechanisms and you have to understand everything, otherwise you can miss anywhere. And if you miss a slight point, the whole thing changes its quality.

Watch—watch passively, not actively. What is the difference?

You are waiting for your girlfriend, or your lover—then you watch actively. Then somebody passes by the door and you jump up to look whether she has come. Then, just leaves fluttering in the wind, and you feel that maybe she has come. You go on jumping up; your mind is very eager, active. No, this will not help. If you are too eager and too active this will not bring you to the silence I am talking about.

Be passive—as you sit by the side of a river and the river floats by and you simply watch. There is no eagerness, no urgency, no emergency. Nobody is forcing you. Even if you miss, there is nothing missed. You simply watch, you just look. Even the word *watch* is not good, because the very word *watch* gives a feeling of being active. You simply look, not having anything to do. You simply sit by the bank of the river, you look, and the river flows by. Or you look in the sky and the clouds float by. And passively—this passiveness is very essential. That is to be understood, because your obsession for activity can become eagerness, can become an active waiting. Then you miss the whole point; then the activity has entered from the back door again. Be a passive watcher—*Empty your mind and think of nought.*

This passivity will automatically empty your mind. Ripples of activity, ripples of mind energy, by and by, will subside, and the whole surface of your consciousness will be without any waves, without any ripples. It becomes like a silent mirror.

Tilopa goes on to say:

Like a hollow bamboo rest at ease with your body.

This is one of Tilopa's special methods. Every master has his own special method through which he has attained and through which he would like to help others. This is Tilopa's specialty: *Like a hollow bamboo rest at ease with your body*—a bamboo, inside completely hollow. When you rest you just feel that you are like a bamboo, inside completely hollow and empty. And in fact this is the case: your body is just like a bamboo and inside it is hollow. Your skin, your bones, your blood—all are part of the bamboo and inside there is space, hollowness.

When you are sitting with a completely silent mouth, inactive, tongue touching the roof of the mouth and silent, not quivering with thoughts—mind watching passively, not waiting for anything in particular—feel like a hollow bamboo. And suddenly infinite energy starts pouring within you. You are filled with the unknown, with the mysterious, with the divine. A hollow bamboo becomes a flute and the divine starts playing it. Once you are empty then there is no barrier for the divine to enter in you.

Try this; this is one of the most beautiful meditations, the meditation of becoming a hollow bamboo. You need not do anything else. You simply become this—and all else happens. Suddenly you feel something is descending in your hollowness. You are like a womb and a new life is entering in you, a seed is falling. And a moment comes when the bamboo completely disappears.

Like a hollow bamboo rest at ease with your body. Rest at ease— don't desire spiritual things, don't desire heaven, don't desire even God. God cannot be desired—when you are desireless, he comes to you. Liberation cannot be desired—because desire is the bondage. When you are desireless you are liberated. Buddhahood cannot be desired, because desiring is the hindrance. When the barrier is not, suddenly the buddha explodes in you. You have the seed already. When you are empty, when the space is there—the seed explodes.

Tilopa says:

Like a hollow bamboo rest at ease with your body. Giving
not nor taking, put your mind at rest.

There is nothing to give, there is nothing to get. Everything is absolutely okay as it is. There is no need for any give and take. You are absolutely perfect as you are.

This teaching of the East has been very much misunderstood in the West, because they say, "What type of teaching is this? Then people will not strive, and then they will not try to go higher. Then

> ❧
>
> The very effort to "become" is a barrier—because you are already carrying your being with you. You need not become anything—simply realize who you are, that's all. Simply realize who is hidden within you.

they will not make any effort to change their character, to transform their evil ways into good ways. Then they may become a victim of the devil." In the West, "Improve yourself" is the slogan—either in terms of this world or in terms of the other, but improve. How to improve? How to become greater and bigger?

In the East we understand it more deeply, that this very effort to "become" is the barrier—because you are already carrying your being with you. You need not become anything—simply realize who you are, that's all. Simply realize who is hidden within you. Improving, whatsoever you improve, you will always be in anxiety and anguish because the very effort to improve is leading you on a wrong path. It makes future meaningful, a goal meaningful, ideals meaningful—and then your mind becomes a desiring.

Desiring, you miss. Let desiring subside, become a silent pool of nondesiring—and suddenly you are surprised, unexpectedly it is there. And you will have a belly laugh, as Bodhidharma laughed. And Bodhidharma's followers say that when you become silent again you can hear his roaring laugh. He is still laughing. He has not stopped laughing since then. He laughed because, "What type of joke is this? You are already that which you are trying to become! How can you be successful if you are already that, and you are trying to become that? Your failure is absolutely certain. How can you become that which you are already?" So Bodhidharma laughed.

Bodhidharma was just exactly a contemporary of Tilopa. They may have known each other—maybe not physically, but they must have known each other, the same quality of being.

Tilopa says:

Giving not nor taking, put your mind at rest. Mahamudra is like a mind that clings to nought.

You have achieved if you don't cling—nothingness in your hand, and you have achieved.

Mahamudra is like a mind that clings to nought. Thus practicing, in time you will reach buddhahood.

What is to be practiced then? To be more and more at ease. To be more and more here and now. To be more and more in action, and less and less in activity. To be more and more hollow, empty, passive. To be more and more a watcher—indifferent, not expecting anything, not desiring anything. To be happy with yourself as you are. To be celebrating.

And then any moment, when things ripen and the right season comes, you bloom into a buddha.

ACT IN HARMONY WITH NATURE

Creativity is a very paradoxical state of consciousness and being. It is action through inaction, it is what Lao Tzu calls *wei-wu-wei*. It is allowing something to happen through you. It is not a doing, it is an allowing. It is becoming a passage so the whole can flow through you. It is becoming a hollow bamboo, just a hollow bamboo.

And then immediately something starts happening, because hidden behind man is God. Just give him a little way, a little passage, to come through you. That is creativity—allowing God to happen is creativity. Creativity is a religious state.

That's why I say that a poet is far closer to God than a theologian, a dancer even closer. The philosopher is the farthest away because the more you think, the greater the wall you create between you and the whole. The more you think, the more you are. The ego is nothing but all the thoughts you have accumulated in the past. When you are not, God is—that is creativity.

Creativity simply means you are in a total relaxation. It does not mean inaction, it means relaxation—because out of relaxation much action will be born. But that will not be your doing, you will be just a vehicle. A song will start coming through you—you are not the creator of it, it comes from the beyond. It always comes from the beyond. When you create it, it is just ordinary, mundane. When it comes *through* you it has superb beauty, it brings something of the unknown in it.

When the great poet Coleridge died he left thousands of poems incomplete. Many times in his life he was asked, "Why don't you

> The more you think, the more you are. The ego is nothing but all the thoughts accumulated in the past. When you are not, God is. That is creativity.

complete these poems," because a few poems were missing only one line or two lines. "Why don't you complete them?"

And he would say, "I cannot. I have tried, but when I complete them something goes amiss, something goes wrong. My line never falls in tune with that which has come through me. It remains a stumbling block, it becomes a rock, it hinders the flow. So I have to wait. Whosoever has been flowing through me, whenever he again starts flowing and completes the poem it will be completed, not before that."

He completed only a few poems. But those are of superb beauty, of great mystic splendor. That has always been so: the poet disappears, then there is creativity. Then he is possessed. Yes, that is the word, he is possessed. To be possessed by God is creativity.

Simone de Beauvoir has said, "Life is occupied both in perpetuating itself and in surpassing itself; if all it does is maintain itself, then living is only not dying." And the man who is not creative is only not dying, that's all. His life has no depth. His life is not yet life but just a preface; the book of life has not yet started. He is born, true, but he is not alive.

When you become creative, when you allow creativity to happen through you—when you start singing a song that is not your own, that you cannot sign and you cannot say, "It is my own," on which you cannot put your signature—then life takes wings, it upsurges. In creativity is the surpassing; otherwise, at the most we

> Nature gives everybody energy which is creative. It becomes destructive only when it is obstructed, when no natural flow is allowed.

can go on perpetuating ourselves. You create a child—it is not creativity. You will die and the child will be here to perpetuate life, but to perpetuate is not enough unless you start surpassing yourself. And this surpassing happens only when something of the beyond comes in contact with you.

That is the point of transcendence—surpassing. And in surpassing, the miracle happens: you are not, and yet for the first time you *are*.

The essence of wisdom is to act in harmony with nature. That is the message of all the great mystics—Lao Tzu, Buddha, Bahauddin, Sosan, Sanai—to act in harmony with nature. Animals act unconsciously in harmony with nature. Man has to act consciously in harmony with nature. Because man has consciousness, man can choose not to act in harmony; hence the great responsibility.

Man has responsibility—only man has responsibility, that is his grandeur. No other animal is responsible; he simply acts in harmony, there is no way of going astray. The animal cannot go astray; he is not yet able to go astray, there is no consciousness yet. He functions as you function in deep sleep.

In deep sleep you also fall in harmony with nature. That's why deep sleep is so rejuvenating, so relaxing. Just a few minutes of deep sleep, and you are fresh and young again. All the dust that you had gathered and all weariness and boredom disappear. You have contacted the source.

But this is an animal way to contact the source; sleep is an animal way to contact the source. Animals are horizontal, man is vertical. When you want to go into sleep you have to fall into a horizontal position. Only in a horizontal position can you fall asleep—you cannot fall asleep standing, it will be very difficult. You have to go back again, millions of years back, just like an animal.

You are horizontal, parallel to the earth; suddenly you start losing consciousness, suddenly you are no longer responsible.

It is because of this factor that Sigmund Freud chose the couch for the patient. It is not for the comfort of the patient, it is a strategy. Once the patient is horizontal he starts being irresponsible. And unless he feels utterly free to say things, he will not say unconscious things. If he remains responsible and vertical he will be continuously judging whether to say a thing or not. He will be censoring. When he is lying horizontal on the couch—and the psychoanalyst is hidden behind, you cannot see him—suddenly he is again like an animal, he has no responsibility. He starts babbling things that he would never have said to anybody, to a stranger. He starts saying things that are deep in his unconscious; those unconscious things start surfacing. It is a strategy, a Freudian strategy to make the patient utterly helpless like a child or like an animal.

Once you don't feel responsible you become natural. And psychotherapy has been of great help; it relaxes you. All that you have repressed surfaces, and after surfacing it evaporates. After going through psychoanalysis you become less burdened, you become more natural, you are more in harmony with nature and with yourself. That is the meaning of being healthy.

But this is going back, this is regression. It is going to the basement. There is another way to surpass, and that is going to the attic—not the way of Sigmund Freud but the way of Buddha. You can surpass yourself by being in contact consciously with nature.

And that is the essence of wisdom—to be in harmony with nature, with the natural rhythm of the universe. And whenever you are in harmony with the natural rhythm of the universe, you are a poet, you are a painter, you are a musician, you are a dancer.

Try it. Sometime, sitting by the side of a tree, fall in tune consciously. Become one with nature, let boundaries dissolve. Become the tree, become the grass, become the wind—and suddenly you will see, something that has never happened to you before is happening. Your eyes are becoming psychedelic: trees are greener than they have ever been, and roses are rosier, and everything seems to be luminous. Suddenly you want to sing a song, not knowing from where it comes. Your feet are ready to dance, you can feel the dance murmuring inside your veins. You can hear the sound of music within and without.

> The essence of wisdom is to be in harmony with nature, with the natural rhythm of the universe. And whenever you are in harmony with the natural rhythm of the universe you are a poet, you are a painter, you are a musician, you are a dancer.

This is the state of creativity. This can be called the basic quality of it—being in harmony with nature, being in tune with life, with the universe.

Lao Tzu has given it a beautiful name, *wei-wu-wei*, action through inaction. That's the paradox of creativity. If you see a painter painting, certainly he is active, utterly active, madly active—he is all action. Or if you see a dancer dancing, he is all action. But still, deep down there is no actor, no doer; there is only silence. Hence I say creativity is a state of paradox.

All beautiful states are paradoxical. The higher you go, the deeper you go into the paradox of reality. Supreme action with supreme relaxation—on the surface great action is happening, in the depth nothing is happening, or *only* nothing is happening. Yielding to a power not your own, surrendering to a power that is beyond you, is creativity. Meditation is creativity. And when the ego disappears the wound in you disappears; you are healed, you are whole—the ego is your disease. And when the ego disappears you are no longer dormant, you start flowing. You start flowing with the immense flow of existence.

Norbert Weiner has said, "We are not stuff that abides, but patterns that perpetuate themselves, whirlpools of water in an ever-flowing river." Then you are not an ego but an event, or a process of events. Then you are a process, not a thing. Consciousness is not a thing, it is a process—and we have made it a thing. The moment you call it "I" it becomes a thing—defined, bounded, dormant, stagnant, and you start dying.

The ego is your death, and the death of the ego is the beginning of your real life. Real life is creativity.

> If you see a painter painting, certainly he is active, utterly active, madly active—he is all action. Or if you see a dancer dancing, he is all action. But still, deep down there is no actor, no doer; there is only silence. Hence I say creativity is a state of paradox.

You need not go to any school to learn creativity. All that you need is to go withinward and help the ego dissolve. Don't support it, don't go on strengthening and nourishing it. And whenever the ego is not, all is truth, all is beautiful. And then whatsoever happens is good.

I am not saying that you all will become Picassos or Shakespeares, I am not saying that. A few of you will become painters, a few of you will become singers, a few of you will become musicians, a few of you dancers—but that is not the point. Each of you will become creative in your own way. You may be a cook, but there will be creativity. Or you may be a street cleaner, but there will be creativity.

There will be no boredom. You will become inventive in small things. Even in cleaning there will be a kind of worship, a prayer, so whatsoever you do then will have the taste of creativity. And we don't need many painters—if all turn out to be painters, life will become very difficult! We don't need many poets; we need gardeners too, we need farmers too, and we need all kinds of people. But each person can be creative. If he is meditative and egoless, then God starts flowing through him. According to his capacities, according to his potential, God starts taking forms—then all is good.

You need not become famous. A really creative person does not care a bit about becoming famous; there is no need. He is so tremendously fulfilled in whatsoever he is doing, he is so content with whatsoever he is and wherever he is, that there is no question of desire. When you are creative, desires disappear. When you are creative, ambitions disappear. When you are creative, you are already that which you always wanted to be.

FIVE OBSTACLES

❧

Nature gives everybody energy that is creative. It becomes destructive only when it is obstructed, when no natural flow is allowed.

1. SELF-CONSCIOUSNESS

Self-consciousness is a disease. Consciousness is health, self-consciousness is disease—something has gone wrong. Some knot has arisen, some complex. The river of consciousness is not flowing naturally. Something foreign has entered into the river of consciousness—something alien, something that cannot be absorbed by the river, something that cannot become part of the river . . . something that resists becoming part of the river.

Self-consciousness is morbidity. Self-consciousness is a frozen state, blocked. It is like a dirty pool—going nowhere, just drying out, evaporating and dying. Of course, it stinks.

So the first thing to be understood is the difference between self-consciousness and consciousness.

Consciousness has no idea of "I," of ego. It has no idea of one's separation from existence. It does not know any barrier. It knows no boundaries—it is one with existence, it is in a deep at-onement.

There is no conflict between the individual and the whole. One is simply flowing into the whole, and the whole is flowing into one. It is like breathing: you breathe in, you breathe out—when you breathe in the whole enters you, when you breathe out you enter the whole. It is a constant flow, a constant sharing. The whole goes on giving to you and you go on giving to the whole. The balance is never lost.

But in a self-conscious man something has gone wrong. He takes in but he never gives out. He goes on accumulating and he has become incapable of sharing. He goes on making boundaries around himself so nobody can trespass. He goes on putting signboards around his being: "No Trespassing Allowed." By and by he becomes a grave, a dead being—because life is in sharing.

A self is a dead thing, alive only in name. Consciousness is infinite life, life abundant. It knows no boundaries. But ordinarily everybody is self-conscious.

To be self-conscious is to be unconscious. This paradox has to be understood: to be self-conscious is to be unconscious and to be unselfconscious—or to be self-unconscious—is to become conscious. And when there is no self, when this small, tiny self disappears, you attain to the real self with a capital *S*—call it the supreme self, the self of all.

So it is both: no-self in the sense that it is not only yours, and the ultimate self also, because it is the self of all. You lose your tiny center and you attain to the center of existence itself. Suddenly you become infinite; suddenly you are no longer bound, you have no cage around your being, and infinite power starts flowing through you. You become a vehicle—clear, with no obstructions. You become a flute, and Krishna can sing through you. You become just a passage, empty, nothing of your own—this is what I call surrender.

Self-consciousness is a nonsurrendering attitude—it is the attitude of conflict, fight, struggle. If you are fighting with existence you will be self-conscious and, of course, you will be defeated again and again and again. Each step is going to be a step into more and more defeat. Your frustration is certain, you are doomed from the very beginning because you cannot maintain this self against the universe. It is impossible, you cannot exist separately. You cannot be a monk.

This word *monk* is good. You must be aware of similar words that come from the same root, like *monopoly* or *monastery* or *monologue.* A monk is one who is trying to be himself, who is trying to define his boundaries and who is trying to exist separate from this total existence. His whole effort is egoistic. It is bound to fail; no monk can ever succeed.

You can succeed only with God, never against him. You can succeed only with the whole, never against it. So if you are frustrated, in deep misery, remember: you are creating that misery. And you are creating it by a subtle trick: you are fighting against the whole.

It happened—it must have been a rainy season like this— and the village river was flooded. People came running to Mulla Nasruddin and said, "Your wife has fallen in the flooded river. Run fast! Save her!"

Nasruddin ran. He jumped into the river and started swimming upstream. The people who had gathered to see, they shouted, "What are you doing, Nasruddin? Your wife cannot go upstream—the stream has taken her downward."

Nasruddin said, "What are you talking about? I know my wife, she can *only* go upstream!"

The ego is always in an effort to go upstream. People don't like to do easy things. Before they can do them they want to make them hard, difficult. People enjoy doing hard things. Why? Because when you face a hard thing, your ego becomes subtle, sharp; there is a challenge.

When the first group reached the top of Everest, somebody asked Edmund Hillary, "Why did you take such a risk? It was dangerous—many others have died before you and have not been able to reach." And the person who was asking was unable to understand why people go on trying to reach Everest and losing their lives. What is the point of it? What is there to achieve?

Edmund Hillary is reported to have said, "We cannot rest as long as this Everest remains unconquered. We have to conquer it!" There is nothing to gain in it, but the very presence of Everest unconquered is a challenge. To whom is it a challenge? To the ego.

> You can succeed only with God, never against him. You can succeed only with the whole, never against it.

Watch your own life—many things you are doing only because of the ego. You want to make a big house—you may be perfectly comfortable in your house as it is, but you want to make a big palace. That big palace is not for you, that big palace is for the ego. You may be perfectly comfortable as you are, but you go on accumulating money—that money is not for you, that money is for the ego. How can you rest unless you have become the richest man in the world?

But what are you going to do by becoming the richest man in the world? You will become more and more miserable, because only misery comes out of conflict. Misery is an indication that you are in conflict. So don't throw your responsibility on something else. People are very good at rationalizing. If they are miserable they will say, "What can we do?—the past lives' karmas are making us miserable." All rubbish! Past life karmas must have made you miserable, but in past lives! Why should they wait till now? There is no point in waiting. Your *present* karmas are making you miserable! Throwing it on past lives makes it easy—what can you do? You have to be the way you are, now nothing can be done. The past cannot be undone, you cannot erase it just by waving your hand. There is no magic trick that can help you to erase your past. It has happened and it has happened forever; now it is going to remain absolute, there is no possibility of changing it. That relieves you of the burden and you think, "So okay, I have to be miserable because of the past karmas."

> People don't like to do easy things. Before they can do them they want to make them hard, difficult. People enjoy doing hard things. Why? Because when you face a hard thing, your ego becomes subtle, sharp, there is a challenge.

You can throw the responsibility on the devil, as Christians go on doing. Hindus go on throwing the responsibility on past karmas, and Christians go on throwing the responsibility on the devil—he must be creating traps for you. It is not you, it is the devil who goes on trapping you into miseries and who goes on pulling you down toward hell.

Who is bothered with you? Why should this devil be bothered with you?

Then there are Marxists, communists, socialists—they say it is the social structure, the economic system that makes people miserable. Then there are Freudians, psychoanalysts; they say it is the child and mother relationship. But it is always something else, it is never you. It is never you in the present.

And I would like to tell you, it is you. If you are miserable, you and only you are responsible. Neither the past nor the social structure nor the economic system—nothing is going to help. If you remain you, in any sort of a society, you will remain miserable. In any economic system you will remain miserable, in any world you will remain miserable—if you remain you.

And the first, basic change happens when you start dropping this conflict with existence. That is the only meaning of all the great religions when they emphasize, "Drop the ego." They are saying, "Drop the conflict." I would like you to remember it more, because "drop the ego" seems too metaphysical. Ego? Where is the ego? What is the ego? The word seems to be known, you seem to be well acquainted with it, but it seems to be very vague, cannot be grasped. I would like to make it more prac-

> Change happens when you start dropping the conflict with existence. That is the only meaning of all the great religions when they emphasize, "Drop the ego." They are saying, "Drop the conflict."

tical: drop the conflict, because ego is a by-product of your conflicting attitude.

People talk of conquering nature, people talk of conquering this and that—how can you conquer nature? You are part of it. How can the part conquer the whole? See the foolishness of it, the stupidity. You can be with the whole in harmony, or you can be in conflict with the whole in disharmony. Disharmony results in misery; harmony results in bliss. Harmony naturally results in a deep silence, joy, delight. Conflict results in anxiety, anguish, stress, tension.

The ego is nothing but all the tensions that you have created around yourself. And in the first place there is no need to create it— but why does man go on creating it? There must be some reason. Why does everybody go on creating the ego, the self? The real self is unknown, that's why. And it is very difficult to live without a self, so we create a pseudoself, a substitute self. The real self is unknown.

In fact, the real self never becomes absolutely known; it remains mysterious, it remains ineffable, indefinable. The real self is so vast that you cannot define it, and the real self is so mysterious that you cannot penetrate it to the very core. The real self is the self of the whole. It is not possible for human intellect to penetrate, to ponder, to contemplate it.

There is a famous story of a wise

> The ego is nothing but all the tensions that you have created around yourself. And in the first place there is no need to create it—but why does man go on creating it? There must be some reason.

man who was called to see Alexander the Great. And Alexander asked him, "I have heard that you have come to know what God is, so please tell me. I have been in search, and people say you have attained, so enlighten me about God, what God is."

It is said the wise man said, "You give me at least twenty-four hours to think over it."

Twenty-four hours passed, and Alexander was waiting very eagerly. The wise man came and he said, "Seven days will be needed."

And then seven days passed, and Alexander was very impatient. The wise man came and he said, "One year will be needed."

Alexander said, "What do you mean, one year will be needed? You know or you don't! If you know, you know—tell me. Why waste time?"

The wise man laughed and he said, "The more I ponder, the more it becomes unknowable. The more I know, the more difficult it becomes to say that I know. Twenty-four hours I tried and tried, and it started slipping from my hands. It is very elusive, it is like mercury. Then I asked for seven days—that didn't help. Now, at least one year—and I am not certain that I will be able to bring a definition."

The wise man did well. He must have been really wise, because there is no way to define the real self. But man cannot live without a self—then one feels so empty! Then one feels like a wheel without a hub, then one feels like a circumference without a center. No, it is hard to live without a self.

To know the real self is arduous; one has to travel long to arrive home. One has to knock on many doors before one comes to the right door. The easy trick is, you can create a false self. To grow real roses is difficult; you can purchase plastic roses. They will not deceive you, but they will deceive the neighbors. Mm? That is the point of the self, the ego. It cannot deceive you—you know well that you yourself don't know who you are—but at least it can deceive the neighbors. In the outside world at least you have a certain label, who you are.

Have you ever thought about it? If somebody asks, "Who are you?" what do you answer? You say your name. The name is not yours, because you came into the world without a name. You came nameless; it is not your property, it has been given to you. And any name, A-B-C-D, would have been useful. It is arbitrary. It is not essential in any way. If you are called "Susan" good; if you are called "Harry" good, it makes no difference. Any name would have been as applicable to you as any other. It is just a label. A name is needed to call you by, but it has nothing to do with your being.

Or you say, "I am a doctor" or you say, "I am an engineer"—or a businessman, or a painter, or this and that—but nothing says anything about you. When you say, "I am a doctor," you say something about your profession, not about you. You say how you earn your living. You don't say anything about life, you say something about your living. You may be earning your living as an engineer, or as a doctor, or as a businessman—it is irrelevant. It does not say anything about you.

> *To grow real roses is difficult; you can purchase plastic roses. They will not deceive you, but they will deceive the neighbors—that is the point of the ego.*

Or you say your father's name, your mother's name, you give your family tree—that too is irrelevant because that doesn't define you. Your being born in a particular family is accidental; you could as well have been born in another family and you would not even have noticed the difference. These are just utilitarian tricks—and man becomes a "self." This self is a pseudoself, a created, manufactured self, homemade. And your own real self remains deep down hidden in mist and mystery.

I was reading:

A Frenchman was crossing the desert with an Arab guide. Day after day, the Arab never failed to kneel on the burning sand and call upon his God. At last, one evening the unbeliever said to the Arab, "How do you know there is a God?"

The guide fixed his eye upon the scoffer for a moment and then replied: "How do I know there is a God? How did I know that a camel and not a man passed last night? Was is not by the print of his hoof in the sand?" And pointing to the sun whose last rays were fading over the horizon, he added, "That footprint is not of man."

Your self cannot be created by you, it cannot be manmade. Your self you have brought with you—it is you, how can you create it? To create it you will have to be there in the first place. That is the meaning when Christians, Mohammedans, Hindus say that man is a "creature." That means that man has not created himself, that's all. The creator is somewhere hidden in the unknown. We have come out of some mysterious life source. Your self is not yours! This false self is not yours because you have created it; and your real self is not yours because it is still in God, you are still rooted in God.

This false self that we go on carrying in our lives like a flag is always in danger of being damaged. It is very fragile, it is very weak—it has to be, it is manmade. How can man make something deathless? He himself has to pass through many deaths, so whatsoever he produces is always mortal. Hence the fear, continuous fear that "I may be lost. My self may be destroyed." A continuous fear goes on trembling in your being—you can never be certain about this false self of yours, you know it is false. You may avoid the fact but you know it is false. It is gathered together, manufactured; it is mechanical, it is not organic.

Have you observed the difference between an organic unity and a mechanical unity? You make a car engine; you can purchase parts from the market and you can assemble those parts, and the engine starts functioning like a unity. Or you can purchase parts of a radio from the market and you can assemble them, and the radio starts functioning like a unity. Somehow it comes to have a self. No part can function as a radio by itself—all parts together start functioning like a radio. But still the unity is mechanical, forced from the outside.

But when you throw seeds into the ground, those seeds die into the soil and a plant arises—this unity is organic. It is not forced from outside, the unity was within the seed itself. The seed goes on spouting, goes on gathering a thousand and one things from the earth, from the air, from the sun, from the sky—but the unity is coming from within. The center comes first and then the circumference. In a mechanical unity the circumference comes first and then the center.

Man is an organic unity. You were a seed one day, like any

tree; in the soil of your mother's womb you started gathering your circumference. The center came first, the center preceded the circumference—and now you have forgotten the center completely. You live on the circumference and you think this is your whole life. This circumference, and continuously living on it, creates a sort of self, a pseudoself, which gives you a feeling that yes, you are somebody. But it is always trembling because it has no organic unity in it.

Hence the fear of death. If you know your real self you will never be afraid of death, there is no question, because the organic unity never dies. Organic unity is immortal. Only mechanical unities are put together and die. That which is put together, one day will fall apart. Mechanical unity has a beginning and an end. The organic unity has no beginning and no end—it is an eternal process.

Do you know your center? If you don't know it then you will be continuously afraid. Hence, self-consciousness is always afraid, always trembling. And you always need support from others—somebody to appreciate you, somebody to clap, somebody to say how beautiful you are or how intelligent. You need somebody to say these things to you, like hypnotic suggestions, so that you can believe that yes, you are intelligent, you are beautiful, you are strong. But see the point: you depend on others.

> Self-consciousness is always afraid, always trembling. And you always need support from others—somebody to appreciate you, somebody to clap, somebody to say how beautiful you are or how intelligent.

A foolish man comes to you and says you are very intelligent—and in fact, you can look intelligent only to a foolish man. If he is more intelligent than you, of course you will not look intelligent to him. So a foolish man comes and certifies your intelligence, and you are very happy. You can look beautiful only to an ugly man. If he is more beautiful than you, you will look ugly—because it is all relative. And you are certified by ugly people that you are beautiful, and you are tremendously happy.

What type of intelligence is this, which has to be certified by foolish people? What type of beauty is this, which has to be certified by ugly people? It is completely false. It is idiotic! But we go on searching. We go on searching in the outside world to find some support for our ego, somebody to give a little support, to become a prop. Otherwise there is always the danger that our ego will collapse. So we have to support it from this side and from that, and continuous worry arises.

That's why you are more graceful when you are alone—because you are not worried. Nobody is there to see you. You are more innocent when you are alone—in your bathroom you are more innocent, you are more like a child. Again you stand before the mirror and make faces, and you enjoy it. But if you become aware that your small child is looking through the keyhole, immediately you are totally different. Now the ego is at stake. That's why people are so much afraid of others. Alone, there is no anxiety.

There is a famous Zen story:

A Zen master was making a painting, and he had his chief disciple sit by his side to tell him when the painting was perfect. The disciple was worried and the master was also worried, because the disciple had never seen the master do anything imperfect. But that day things started going wrong. The master tried, and the more he tried, the more it was a mess.

In Japan or in China, the whole art of calligraphy is done on rice paper, on a certain very sensitive paper, very fragile. If you hesitate a little, for centuries it can be known where the calligrapher hesitated—because more ink spreads into the rice paper and makes it a mess. It is very difficult to deceive on rice paper. You have to go on flowing; you are not to hesitate. Even for a single moment, a split second, if you hesitate—what to do?—you have missed, already missed. And one who has a keen eye will immediately say, "It is not a Zen painting at all," because a Zen painting has to be a spontaneous painting, flowing.

The master tried and tried and the more he tried . . . he started perspiring. And the disciple was sitting there and shaking his head again and again negatively, "No, this is not perfect." And more and more mistakes were being made by the master.

Then the ink was running out so the master said, "You go out and prepare more ink." While the disciple was outside preparing the ink, the master did his masterpiece. When the disciple came back in he said, "Master, but this is perfect! What happened?"

The master laughed. He said, "I became aware of one thing— your presence, the very idea that somebody is there to appreciate or to condemn, to say no or yes, disturbed my inner tranquility. Now I will never be disturbed. I have come to know that I was trying to make it perfect and that was the only reason for its not being perfect."

Try to make something perfect and it will remain imperfect. Do it naturally and it is always perfect. Nature is perfect; effort is imperfect. So whenever you are doing something too much, you are destroying.

That's why it happens that everybody talks so beautifully—everybody is a talker, people talk their whole life—but just put them on a platform and tell them to talk to a crowd and suddenly they become dumb; suddenly they forget everything, suddenly they cannot utter a single word. Or even if they do speak, it is not graceful, it is not natural, it is not flowing. What has happened? And you have known this man talking so beautifully to his friends, to his wife, to his children. These are also people, the same people—why are you afraid? You have become self-conscious. Now the ego is at stake, you are trying to perform something.

> Try to make something perfect and it will remain imperfect. Do it naturally and it is always perfect. Nature is perfect, effort is imperfect. So whenever you are doing something too much, you are destroying it.

Listen carefully: whenever you try to perform something, you are seeking food for the ego. Whenever you are natural and let things happen they are perfect, and then there is no problem. When you are natural and let things happen, God is behind you. When you are afraid, trembling, trying to prove something, you have lost God. In your fear, you have forgotten him. You are looking more at the people and you have forgotten your source.

Self-consciousness becomes a weakness. A person who is unselfconscious is strong, but his strength has nothing to do with himself—it comes from the beyond.

When you are self-conscious you are in trouble. When you are self-conscious you are really showing symptoms that you don't know who you are. Your very self-consciousness indicates that you have not come home yet.

It happened:

As a pretty girl passed by, Mulla Nasruddin turned to look. His wife said with a pout, "Every time you see a pretty girl you forget you are married."

"That's where you are wrong," said the Mulla. "Nothing makes me more aware of the fact!"

Whenever you are self-conscious you are simply showing that you are not conscious of the self at all. You don't know who you are. If you had known, then there would have been no problem— then you are not seeking opinions. Then you are not worried what others say about you—it is irrelevant! In fact, nobody ever says anything about you—whenever people say something about you, they are saying it about themselves.

One day it happened: I was in Jaipur and a man came in the morning to see me, and he said, "You are divine."

I said, "You are right!"

He was sitting there and another man came and he was very much against me, and then he said, "You are almost devilish."

I said, "You are right!"

> When you are self-conscious you are really showing symptoms that you don't know who you are. Your very self-consciousness indicates that you have not come home yet.

54

The first man became a little worried. He said, "What do you mean? You told me also, 'You are right,' and you say to this man also, 'You are right'—we can't be both right."

I told him, "Not only two—millions of people can be right about me, because whatsoever they say about me they say about themselves. How can they know me? It is impossible—they have not even known themselves yet. Whatsoever they say is their interpretation."

So the man said, "Then who are you? If this is my interpretation that you are divine, and this is his interpretation that you are evil, then who are you?"

I said, "I am just myself. I have no interpretation about myself, and there is no need. I am simply delighted in being myself, whatsoever that means. I am happy in being myself."

Nobody can say anything about you. Whatsoever people say is about themselves. But you become very shaky, because you are still clinging to a false center. That false center depends on others, so you are always looking to what people are saying about you. And you are always following other people, you are always trying to satisfy them. You are always trying to be respectable, you are always trying to decorate your ego. This is suicidal.

Rather than being disturbed by what others say, you should start looking inside yourself. To know the real self is not so cheap. But people are always hankering for cheap things.

It happened:

When the pain in Mulla Nasruddin's back became unbearable, he reluctantly went to a specialist to diagnose his problem.

"Well," said the doctor, "your problem can be cured

by an operation, two weeks in the hospital and six months totally horizontal.''

"Doctor, I can't afford the cost of all that!" shouted Nasruddin.

"Well then, for twenty-five dollars I can retouch the X ray," suggested the doctor.

This is cheap!—retouch the X ray—but it is not going to make you healthy. That's what we are doing, continuously retouching the X ray and thinking that somehow the miracle will happen. When you are decorating your ego you are retouching the X ray. That is not going to help in any way, it is not going to help you become healthy. It is cheaper—no operation is needed, no expense is involved. But what is the point? Your misery remains.

You become respectable and your misery remains. You become highly praised by the society—your misery remains. You are decorated with gold medals but your misery remains. These gold medals are not going to destroy your misery; they are like retouching the X ray. All decoration on the ego, for the ego, is nothing but deceiving yourself. And you go on becoming weaker and weaker and weaker because the ego goes on becoming weaker every day. Your body will become weaker, your mind will become weaker, and by and by the ego that you have created out of the body and mind combination will become weaker. Fear will become greater and greater; you will be sitting on a volcano that can any day explode. It will not allow you rest. It will not allow you relaxation, it will not allow you any moments of peace.

Once you understand it then the whole energy is put into another direction. One has to know oneself. One has not to be worried about what others say about you.

A friend has sent me a very beautiful joke:

There was this guy, and nobody ever noticed him, he did not have any friends. He was at a salesman's convention in Miami, and he saw that everybody else was happy and laughing and paying attention to each other, but not to him.

One evening he was sitting really bummed out when he got to talking with another salesman. He told him his problem. "Oh, I know how to fix that up," cried the other. "You just get a camel and ride it around in the streets, and in no time everybody will notice you and you will have all the friends you want."

As fate would have it, there was a circus going out of business and they wanted to sell a camel. The man bought it and rode up and down the streets on it, and, sure enough, everybody paid attention to him and noticed him. He felt on top of the world. But then a week later, the camel disappeared. The man was heartbroken and immediately phoned the local newspaper to place an ad for his lost camel.

"Is it a boy or a girl camel?" inquired the guy on the phone.

"A boy or a girl? How should I know?" raged the man. Then he thought, "Oh, yeah, of course, it was a boy, that's right."

"How do you know?" inquired the adman.

"Because," said the man, "every time I rode up and down the streets people yelled, 'Look at that schmuck on the camel!' "

Schmuck is a Yiddish word, a very beautiful word. It has two meanings, and very relevant—one meaning is "idiot" and another meaning, in the beginning looks very far-fetched, means the male genital organ. But in a way both meanings are very deeply related. Idiots live only as sexual beings—they don't know any other life. So *schmuck* is beautiful. If a person has known only sex as life he is stupid, he is an idiot.

The ego is very deceptive. It goes on hearing what it wants to hear. It goes on interpreting what it wants to interpret, it never sees the fact. It never allows the fact to reveal itself to you. People who live in the ego live behind curtains. And those curtains are not inactive—they are active curtains; whatsoever passes through the curtain, the curtain changes it.

People go on living in a mental world of their own creation. Ego is the center of their world, of the false world—call it *maya*, "illusion"—and around the ego they go on creating a world . . . which is nobody else's world. Only they live in that world.

When you drop the ego, you drop a whole world that you have created around it. For the first time you are able to see things as they are, not as you would like them to be. And when you are capable of knowing the facts of life, you become capable of knowing the truth.

Now a Zen story:

A wrestler named O-Nami, "great waves," was immensely strong and highly skilled in the art of wrestling. In private he defeated even his very teacher, but in public his own young pupils could throw him.

In his trouble he went to a Zen master who was stopping at a nearby temple by the sea, and asked for counsel.

"Great Waves is your name," said the master, "so stay in this temple tonight and listen to the waves of the sea. Imagine you are those waves, forget you are a wrestler and become those huge waves sweeping everything before them."

O-Nami remained. He tried to think only of the waves, but he thought of many things. Then gradually he did think only of the waves. They rolled larger and larger as the night wore on. They swept away the flowers in the vases before the Buddha, they swept away the vases. Even the bronze Buddha was swept away. By dawn the temple was only surging water, and O-Nami sat there with a faint smile on his face.

That day he entered the public wrestling contest and won every bout, and from that day no one in Japan could ever throw him.

This is a story of self-consciousness and how to lose it, and how to drop it, and how to get rid of it. We will try to enter into it step by step.

A wrestler named O-Nami, "great waves," was immensely strong. . . .

Everybody is immensely strong. You don't know your strength, that is another matter. Everybody is immensely strong—has to be, because

When you drop the ego, you drop a whole world that you have created around it. For the first time you are able to see things as they are— not as you would like them to be.

> ❧
>
> Searching for prestige, political authority, what are you searching? You are searching power, strength—and strength is all the time available just by the corner. You are searching in wrong places.

everybody is rooted in God, everybody is rooted in this universe. However small you may look, you are not small—you cannot be by the very nature of things.

Now physicists say that in a small atom so much energy is confined—Hiroshima and Nagasaki were destroyed by atomic energy. And the atom is so small—nobody has yet seen it! It is just an inference, a deduction; nobody has seen the atom. With all the sophisticated instruments science has today, nobody has seen the atom—so small, and such vast energy.

If the atom can have so much energy, what to say about man? What to say about this small flame of consciousness in man? If some day this small flame bursts forth, it is bound to become an infinite source of energy and light. That's how it has happened to a Buddha, or to a Jesus.

Everybody is immensely strong because everybody is immensely divine. Everybody is strong because everybody is rooted in God, in the very origin of existence. Remember it.

The human mind tends to forget it. When you forget it, you become weak. When you become weak you start trying to find some artificial ways to become strong. That's what millions of people are doing. Searching for money, what are you really searching? You are searching power, you are searching strength. Searching for prestige, political authority, what are you searching? You are searching power, strength—and strength is all the time available just by the corner. You are searching in wrong places.

A wrestler named O-Nami, "great waves" . . .

We are all great waves of the ocean. We may have forgotten it, but the ocean has not forgotten us. We may have so much forgotten it that we have no idea of what an ocean is—still, we are in the ocean. Even if a wave forgets and becomes oblivious of the ocean, it is still in the ocean—because the wave cannot exist without the ocean. The ocean can exist without the wave—maybe it can exist without the wave—but the wave cannot exist without the ocean. The wave is nothing but a waving of the ocean; it is a process, it is not an entity. It is just the ocean delighting in its being. God in his delight peoples the earth; God in his delight peoples existence. It is ocean searching ocean, just playful—it has tremendous energy—what to do with it?

A wrestler named O-Nami, "great waves," was immensely strong . . .

But this strength is possible only when the wave knows that it is a wave of a great, infinite ocean. If the wave forgets this, then the wave is very weak. And our "forgetory" is tremendous; our memory is very small, very tiny—forgetory, tremendous. We go on forgetting, and that which is very obvious we forget very easily.

That which is very close we forget very easily. That which is always available we forget very easily.

Do you remember your breathing? You remember only when there is some trouble—you have a cold, breathing trouble, or something; otherwise, who remembers breathing? That's why people remember God only when they are in trouble. Otherwise, who remembers? And God is closer than your breathing, closer than you are to yourself. One tends to forget. Have you watched it? If you don't have something, you remember. When you have it you forget, you take it for granted. Because God cannot be lost, it is very difficult to remember. Only very rare people become capable of remembering God. To remember that which we have never been away from is very difficult.

A fish in the ocean forgets the ocean. Throw the fish on the shore, in the sands, hot sands, and then the fish knows. Then the fish remembers. But there is no way to throw you out of God; there is no shore to him—God is a shoreless ocean. And you are not like a fish, you are like a wave. You are exactly like God; your nature and God's nature are the same.

That's the symbolic meaning of choosing this name for this story.

He was highly skilled in the art of wrestling. In private he
defeated even his teacher . . .

But in private, because in private he must have been capable of forgetting his self.

Remember this sutra. When you remember yourself, you forget God; when you forget yourself, you remember God—and you cannot remember both together. When the wave thinks of herself as a wave she forgets that she is an ocean. When the wave knows herself as the ocean, how can she remember herself now as a wave? Only one is possible: Either the wave can think about herself as a wave, or as the ocean. It is a gestalt; you cannot remember both together, that is impossible.

In private he defeated even his very teacher, but in public
his own young pupils could throw him.

In privacy he must have been completely forgetful of his own self, the ego. Then he was tremendously powerful. In public he must have become too self-conscious. Then he was weak. Self-consciousness is weakness. Self-forgetfulness is strength.

In his trouble he went to a Zen master who was stopping
at a nearby temple by the sea, and asked for counsel.
    "Great Waves is your name," said the master, "so stay
in this temple tonight and listen to the waves of the sea."

A master is one who can create devices for everybody. A master is one who has no fixed device. He looks at the man, this man O-Nami—"Great Waves"—just his name, and he creates a device around his name. Just coming to know that his name is O-Nami, Great Waves, the master said, "Great Waves is your name, so stay in this temple tonight and listen to the waves of the sea."
    Listening is one of the basic secrets of entering into the temple of God. Listening means passivity. Listening means forgetting your-self completely—only then can you listen. When you listen atten-tively to somebody, you forget yourself. If you cannot forget yourself, you never listen. If you are too self-conscious about your-

self, you simply pretend that you are listening—you don't listen. You may nod your head; you may sometimes say yes and no—but you are not listening.

When you listen, you become just a passage—a passivity, a receptivity, a womb. You become feminine. And to arrive, one has to become feminine. You cannot reach God as aggressive invaders, conquerors. You can reach God only . . . or it will be better to say God can reach you only when you are receptive, a feminine receptivity. When you become yin, a receptivity, the door is open. And you wait.

Listening is the art for becoming passive. Buddha has emphasized listening so much, Mahavir has emphasized listening so much, Krishnamurti goes on emphasizing right listening so much. The ears are symbolic. Have you noticed? Your ears are nothing but passages, just holes, nothing else. Your ears are more feminine than your eyes; your eyes are more male. Your ears are yin, your eyes are yang. When you look at somebody you are aggressive, when you listen to somebody you are receptive.

> When you listen attentively to somebody, you forget yourself. If you cannot forget yourself, you never listen. If you are too self-conscious about yourself, you simply pretend that you are listening—you don't listen.

That's why looking at somebody for too long a time becomes vulgar, impolite, unmannerly. There is a certain limit; psychologists say three seconds. If you look at a person for three seconds it's okay; it can be tolerated. More than that, then you are not looking—you are staring, you are offending the person; you are trespassing. But listening to a person has no limit, because ears cannot trespass. They simply remain wherever they are.

Eyes need rest. Have you noticed? In the night the eyes need res. Ears need no rest; they are open twenty-four hours, year in, year out. Eyes cannot remain open even for minutes—continually blinking, continually resting. Aggression tires, because aggression takes your energy out, so the eyes have to blink continually, to rest. The ears are rested always.

That's why music has been used by many religions as an approach toward prayer—because music will make your ears more vibrant, more sensitive. One has to become more of the ears and less of the eyes.

"You just become ears," said the master. "You just listen. There is nothing else to do—just go on listening with no idea why, with no idea of what is happening. Just go on listening with no interpretation, with no activity on your part." And then, *"Imagine you are those waves."*

First listen, get in tune with the waves, and when you feel that now you are completely silent and receptive, then imagine that you are those waves. That is the second step. First, don't be aggressive; become receptive. And when you have become re-

> ☙
>
> The first step is receptivity, because in receptivity ego cannot exist—it can exist only in conflict. And when you are receptive, suddenly your faculty of imagination becomes tremendously powerful.

ceptive, then just melt into those waves, start imagining that you are those waves.

The master is giving him a device so that he can forget his self, the ego. First step is receptivity, because in receptivity ego cannot exist—it can exist only in conflict. And when you are receptive, suddenly your faculty of imagination becomes tremendously powerful.

Receptive people, sensitive people, are imaginative people. Those who can see the greenery of the trees, just without any aggression on their part, not even a subtle aggression on their part— who can just drink the greenery of the trees, who can simply absorb it as if they are sponges—they become very creative, they become very imaginative. These are the poets, the painters, the dancers, the musicians—they absorb the universe in deep receptivity and then they pour whatsoever they have absorbed into their imagination.

> These are the poets, the painters, the dancers, the musicians— they absorb the universe in deep receptivity, and then they pour whatsoever they have absorbed into their imagination.

Imagination is the one faculty you have that comes closest to God. God must have a great imagination, mm?—just look at his world. Just to think!—such an imaginative world, with so many flowers and so many butterflies and so many trees and so many rivers, and so many people. Just think about his imagination! With so many stars, and so many worlds— worlds beyond worlds, nonending . . . He must be a great dreamer.

In the East, Hindus say the world

is God's dream, his imagination. The world is his magic, his imagination. He is dreaming it, we are part of his dream.

When the master said to O-Nami, "Then you imagine yourself as those waves," he was saying, "Then you become creative. First you become receptive and then you become creative." And once you have dropped your ego you become so flexible that whatsoever you imagine will happen. Then your imagination will become your reality.

"Forget you are a wrestler and become those huge waves sweeping everything before them."

O-Nami remained. He tried to think only of the waves . . .

Of course, it was difficult in the beginning, *he thought of many things.* It is natural—but he remained. He must have been very patient. *Then gradually he did think only of the waves.* Then a moment came. . . . If you pursue, if you persist, one moment is bound to come when the thing that you have been desiring for many lives happens—but patience is needed.

Then gradually he did think only of the waves. They rolled larger and larger as the night wore on.

> Only a creative person knows how to drop boredom, the creative person knows no boredom at all. He is thrilled, enchanted, he is constantly in a state of adventure.

> ❧
>
> First you become
> receptive and then
> you become creative.
> And once you have
> dropped your ego,
> you become so
> flexible that
> whatsoever you
> imagine will happen.
> Then your
> imagination will
> become your reality.

These are not the real waves of the ocean that are rolling larger and larger. Now there is no distinction between his waves of imagination and the real waves. That distinction is lost. Now he does not know what is what; what is dream and what is real, he does not know. He has become a small child again. Only children have that capacity.

In the morning you can find a child weeping for a toy he had seen in the dream, and he wants it back, and he says, "Where is my toy?" And you go on insisting that it was just a dream, but he says, "Still, where is it now?"

He makes no distinction between the dream and the waking. He knows no distinctions. He knows reality as one.

When you become very receptive, you become childlike. Now these waves:

They rolled larger and larger as the night wore on. They swept away the flowers in the vases before the Buddha, they swept away the vases. Not only that: Even the bronze Buddha was swept away.

This is beautiful! It is very difficult for a Buddhist to imagine that the Buddha is being swept away. If he had been too much attached to his religion, that would have been the point where he would have been completely cut off from his imagination. He would have said, "Enough is enough! Buddha being swept away?— what am I doing? No, I am no longer a wave." He would have stopped at the feet of the Buddha, he would have touched the feet of the Buddha, but not more than that. But remember, one day, even those feet that have helped you tremendously on the path, they have to go. Buddhas also have to be swept away, because the door can become a hindrance if you cling to it.

> Larger and larger . . . they swept away the flowers in the vases before the Buddha, they swept away the vases. Even the bronze Buddha was swept away. By dawn the temple was only surging water . . .

Not that it really happened—it happened to O-Nami. Remember it: if you had been in that temple during that time you would not have seen the surging water in the temple—it was happening only to O-Nami. It was happening in a totally different dimension of his being. It is the dimension of poetry, imagination, dream—the intuitive, the feminine, the childlike, innocence. He had opened the doors of his imaginative faculty. By listening to the waves, by becoming receptive, he became imaginative. His imagination flowered as a thousand-and-one-petaled lotus.

> By dawn the temple was only surging water, and O-Nami sat there with a faint smile on his face.

He became a buddha! The same faint smile that one day came to Buddha under the bodhi tree must have come to O-Nami. Suddenly he was no more—and that was the smile, the smile of coming back home. The smile that one has arrived, the smile that now there is no longer anywhere to go. The smile that one has reached the source, the smile that one has died and is resurrected.

O-Nami sat there with a faint smile on his face.

That day he entered the public wrestling contest and won every bout, and from that day no one in Japan could ever throw him.

Because now it is not his energy. He is no more O-Nami—he is no more the waves, he is the ocean now. How can you defeat the ocean? You can only defeat the waves.

Once you have dropped the ego you have dropped all defeat, all failure, all frustration. Carry the ego and you are doomed to failure. Carry the ego and you will remain weak. Drop the ego and infinite strength starts flowing through you. By dropping the ego you become a river, you start flowing, you start melting, you start streaming—you become alive.

All life is of the whole. If you are trying to live on your own, you are simply being stupid. It is as if a leaf on a tree is trying to live on its own—not only that, but fighting the tree, fighting other leaves, fighting the roots, thinking that those are all inimical to him. We are just leaves on a tree, a great tree—call it God, or the whole, or you name it, but we are small leaves on an infinite tree of life. There is no need to fight. The only way to come home is to surrender.

2. PERFECTIONISM

I have heard one beautiful story. Once there was a great sculptor, a painter, a great artist. His art was so perfect that when he would make a statue of a man, it was difficult to say who was the man and who was the statue. It was so lifelike, so alive, so similar.

An astrologer told him that his death was approaching, he was going to die soon. Of course, he became very much afraid and frightened, and as every man wants to avoid death he also wanted to avoid it. He thought about it, meditated, and he found a solution. He made statues of himself, eleven in number, and when Death knocked on his door and the Angel of Death entered, he stood hidden among his own eleven statues. He stopped his breathing.

The Angel of Death was puzzled, could not believe his own eyes. It had never happened—it was so irregular! God has never been known to create two persons alike; he always creates the unique. He has never believed in any routine, he is not like an assembly line. He is absolutely against carbons, he creates only originals. What has happened? Twelve persons in all, absolutely alike? Now, whom to take away? Only one has to be taken . . .

The Angel of Death could not decide. Puzzled, worried, nervous, he went back. He asked God, "What have you done? There are twelve persons exactly alike, and I am supposed to bring only one. How should I choose?"

God laughed. He called the Angel of Death close to him, and he uttered the formula in his ear, the key to finding the real among the unreal. He gave him a secret code and told him, "Just go, and utter it in that room where that artist is hiding himself among his own statues."

The Angel of Death asked, "How is it going to work?"

God said, "Don't be worried. Just go and try."

The Angel of Death went, not yet believing it was going to work, but when God has said it he has to do it. He went into the room, looked around and, not addressing anybody in particular, he said, "Sir, everything is perfect except one thing. You have done well, but you have missed one point. One error is there."

The man completely forgot that he was hiding. He jumped, he said, "What error?"

Death laughed. And Death said, "You are caught! This is the only error: you cannot forget yourself. Come on, follow me."

ORDINARILY, THE ARTIST IS THE MOST EGOISTIC PERSON IN THE WORLD. But then he is not a true artist. He has used art as a means for his ego trip. Artists are very egoistic, constantly bragging about themselves and constantly fighting with each other; everybody thinks that he is the first and the last. But this is not true art.

The true artist disappears utterly. These other people are only technicians; I will not call them artists but technicians. I will not call them creators, I will call them only composers. Yes, to compose a poem is one thing, to create a poem is quite another. To compose poetry one needs to know language, grammar, rules of poetics. It is a game with words and if you know the whole game, you can create poetry. It will not be very poetic, but it will have the appearance of poetry. Technically it may be perfect, but it will have only the body—the soul will be missing.

The soul happens only when the artist disappears into his art—he is no longer separate. When the painter paints with such abandon that he is not there, so that he even feels guilty to sign his painting because he knows he has not done it . . . Some unknown force has done it through him, he knows that he has been possessed. That has been the experience of all the really great artists down the ages: the feeling of being possessed. The greater the artist, the more clear the feeling is.

And those who are the greatest— a Mozart, a Beethoven, a Kalidas, a Rabindranath Tagore—those who are the greatest are absolutely certain that they have been nothing but hollow bamboos and existence has been singing through them. They have been flutes but the song is not theirs. It has flowed through them, but it comes from some unknown source. They have not hindered—that's all they have done—but they have not created it.

This is the paradox. The real creator knows that he has not created anything. Existence has worked through him. It has possessed him, his hands, his being, and it has created something through him. He has been instrumental. This is real art, where the artist disappears. Then there is no question of ego. And then art becomes religiousness. Then the artist

> The soul happens only when the artist disappears into his art—he is no longer separate. Some unknown force has done it through him, he knows that he has been possessed. That has been the experience of all the really great artists down the ages, the feeling of being possessed. The greater the artist, the clearer the feeling is.

is a mystic—not only technically right but existentially authentic.

The less of the artist is in his work, the more perfect it is. When the artist is absolutely absent, then the creativity is absolutely perfect—in this proportion, you have to remember. The more the artist is present the less perfect the product will be. If the artist is too much present, the product will be nauseating, it will be neurotic. It will be just ego—what else can it be?

Ego is neurosis. And one thing more to be remembered: ego always wants to be perfect. Ego is very perfectionistic. Ego always wants to be higher and better than others; hence it is perfectionist. But through ego perfection is never possible, so the effort is absurd.

Perfection is possible only when the ego is not—but then one never thinks of perfection at all.

So the real artist never thinks of perfection. He has no idea of perfection, he simply allows himself into a surrender, into a let go, and whatsoever happens, happens. The real artist thinks certainly of totality but never of perfection. He wants to be totally in it, that's all. When he dances, he wants to disappear into the dance. He does not want to be there, because the presence of the dancer will be a disturbance in the dance. The grace, the flow, will be disturbed, obstructed. When the dancer is not there, all rocks have disappeared, the flow is very silent, smooth.

The real artist certainly thinks of totality—how to be total?—

> The less of the artist is in his work, the more perfect it is. When the artist is absolutely absent, then the creativity is absolutely perfect—in this proportion, you have to remember.

but never thinks of perfection. And the beauty is that those who are total are perfect. Those who think of perfection are never perfect, never total. On the contrary, the more they think of perfection the more neurotic they become. They have ideals. They are always comparing and they are always falling short!

If you have an ideal, that unless this ideal is fulfilled you will not think yourself perfect, how can you be total in your act? If you think, for example, that you have to be a dancer like Nijinsky, then how can you be total in your dance? You are constantly looking, watching yourself, trying to improve, afraid to commit any fault. You are divided—a part of you is dancing, another part of you is there, judgmental, standing by the side condemning, criticizing. You are divided, you are split.

> ⪼
>
> The real artist thinks certainly of totality, but never of perfection. He wants to be totally in it, that's all. When he dances, he wants to disappear into the dance.

Nijinsky was perfect because he was total. It used to happen that when he danced and he would take leaps in his dance, people could not believe their eyes; even scientists could not believe their eyes. His leap was such that it was against the law of gravitation—it should not happen! And when he came back to the ground he would come so slowly, like a feather . . . that too is against the law of gravitation.

He was asked about it again and again. The more people asked, the more he became conscious of it, the more it started disappearing. A moment came in his life when it stopped completely, and the reason was that he became conscious of it—he lost his totality. Then he understood it, why it had disappeared. It used to happen, but it used to happen only when Nijinsky was completely lost into the dance. In that complete loosening, in that complete relaxation, one functions in a totally different world, according to different laws.

Let me tell you about one law, which sooner or later science is going to discover. I call it the law of grace. Just as there is a law of gravitation . . . three hundred years ago it was not known. It was functioning even before it was known; a law need not be known in order to function. The law was always functioning; it has nothing to do with Newton and the apple falling from the tree. Apples used to fall before Newton, too! It is not that Newton discovered the law and then the apples started falling. The law was there, Newton discovered it.

Exactly like that, another law is there—the law of grace, which uplifts. The law of gravitation pulls things downward; the law of grace lifts things upward. In yoga they call it levitation. In a certain state of abandon, in a certain state of drunkenness—drunk with the divine—in a certain state of utter surrender, egolessness, that law starts functioning. One is uplifted. One becomes weightless.

That was happening in Nijinsky's case. But you cannot make it happen, because if you are there it will not happen.

Ego is like a rock around your neck. When the ego is not there, you are weightless. And have you not felt it sometimes in your own life? There are moments when you have a kind of weightlessness. You walk on the earth but still your feet don't touch the earth, you are six inches above. Moments of joy, moments of prayer, moments of meditation, moments of celebration, moments of love . . . and you are weightless, you are uplifted.

And I say that sooner or later science will have to discover it, because science believes in a certain principle: the principle of polar opposites. No law can be alone, it must have its opposite. Electricity cannot function with only one pole, positive or negative; both are needed. They complement each other.

Science knows it, that each law has its opposite to complement it. Gravitation must have a law opposite to it, to complement it. That law, tentatively, I call grace— any other name may be possible in the future because scientists, if they discover it, will not call it grace. But that seems to be the most perfect name for it.

3. INTELLECT

"Contemporary mind" is a contradiction in terms. Mind is never contemporary, it is always old. Mind is past—past and past and nothing else. Mind means memory, there can be no contemporary mind. To be contemporary is to be without mind.

If you are herenow, then you are contemporary. But then, don't you see, your mind disappears! No thought moves, no desire arises; you become disconnected with the past and disconnected with the future.

There are moments when you walk on the earth but still your feet don't touch the earth—you are six inches above. Moments of joy, moments of prayer, moments of meditation, moments of celebration, moments of love … and you are weightless, you are uplifted.

Mind is never original, cannot be. No-mind is original, fresh, young; mind is always old, rotten, stale.

But those words are used—they are used in a totally different sense. In that sense, those words are meaningful. The mind of the nineteenth century was a different mind; the questions they were asking, you are not asking. The questions that were very important in the eighteenth century are now stupid questions. "How many angels can dance on the head of a pin?" was one of the greatest theological questions in the Middle Ages. Now can you find such a stupid person who will think that this is an important question?

> *Mind is past—past and past and nothing else. Mind means memory, there can be no contemporary mind. To be contemporary is to be without mind.*

And this was discussed by the greatest theologians; not small people, great professors were writing treatises on it. Conferences were arranged. "How many angels . . . ?" Now, who cares? It is simply irrelevant.

In Buddha's time a great question was, "Who created the world?" It has persisted for centuries, but now fewer and fewer people are worried about who created the world. Yes, there are some old-fashioned people, but very rarely such questions are asked of me. But Buddha encountered it every day; not a single day must have passed when somebody did not ask the question, "Who created the world?" Buddha had to say again and again that the world has always been there, nobody has created it; but people were not satisfied. Now nobody cares. Very rarely somebody asks me the question, "Who created the world?" In that sense, the mind goes on changing as time goes on changing. In that sense, the contemporary mind is a reality.

Husband to wife: "I said we are not going out tonight, and that is semifinal." Now *this* is a contemporary mind. No husband in the past would have said that. It was always final; the last word was his.

Two high-class English ladies met each other by accident while out shopping in London. One noticed the other was pregnant and asked, "Why, darling, what a surprise! You obviously got married since I last saw you!"

The second said, "Yes. He's a wonderful man, he's an officer in the Ghurka rifles."

The questioner was horrified. "A Ghurka! Darling, aren't they all black?"

"Oh no," she said. "Only the privates."

The questioner exclaimed, "Darling, how contemporary!"

In that sense, there is a contemporary mind. Otherwise, there is no contemporary mind. Fashions come and go; if you think of fashions then there are changes. But basically all mind is old. Mind as such is old, and there can be no modern mind; the most modern mind is still of the past.

The really alive person is a herenow person. He does not live out of the past, he does not live for the future; he lives only in the moment, for the moment. The moment is all. He is spontaneous; that spontaneity is the fragrance of no-mind. Mind is repetitive, mind always moves in circles. Mind is a mechanism: you feed it with knowledge, it repeats the same knowledge. It goes on chewing the same knowledge again and again.

No-mind is clarity, purity, innocence. No-mind is the real way to live, the real way to know, the real way to be.

INTELLECT IS SOMETHING PSEUDO, SOMETHING FALSE: it is a substitute for intelligence. Intelligence is a totally different phenomenon—the real thing.

Intelligence needs tremendous courage, intelligence needs an adventurous life. Intelligence needs that you are always going into the unknown, into the uncharted sea. Then intelligence grows, it becomes sharpened. It grows only when it encounters the unknown every moment. People are afraid of the unknown, people feel insecure with the unknown. They don't want to go beyond the familiar; hence they have created a false, plastic substitute for intelligence—they call it intellect.

Intellect is only a mental game. It cannot be creative.

You can go and look in the universities and see what kind of creative work goes on there. Thousands of treatises are being written; PhDs, DLitts, great degrees are conferred on people. Nobody ever comes to know what happens to their PhD theses; they go on becoming rubbish heaps in the libraries. Nobody ever reads them, nobody is ever inspired by them—yes, a few people read them; they are the

> The really alive person is a herenow person. He does not live out of the past, he does not live for the future, he lives only in the moment, for the moment. The moment is all.

same type of people who are going to write another thesis. The would-be PhDs will of course be reading them.

But your universities don't create Shakespeares, Miltons, Dostoevskys, Tolstoys, Rabindranaths, Kahlil Gibrans. Your universities create just junk, utterly useless. This is intellectual activity that goes on in the universities.

Intelligence creates a Picasso, a Van Gogh, a Mozart, a Beethoven. Intelligence is a totally different dimension. It has nothing to do with the head; it has something to do with the heart. Intellect is in the head; intelligence is a state of heart wakefulness. When your heart is awake, when your heart is dancing in deep gratitude, when your heart is in tune with existence, in harmony with existence, out of that harmony is creativity.

There is no possibility of any intellectual creativity. It can produce rubbish—it is productive, it can manufacture—but it cannot create. And what is the difference between manufacturing and creating? Manufacturing is a mechanical activity. Computers can do it—they are already doing it, and doing it in a far more efficient way than you can hope from man. Intelligence creates, it does not manufacture. Manufacturing means a repetitive exercise: what has already been done, you go on doing again and again. Creativity

> People are afraid of the unknown, people feel insecure with the unknown. They don't want to go beyond the familiar; hence they have created a false, plastic substitute for intelligence—they call it intellect. Intellect is only a mental game. It cannot be creative.

means bringing the new into existence, making a way for the unknown to penetrate the known, making a way for the sky to come to the earth.

When there is a Beethoven or a Michelangelo or a Kalidas, the skies open, flowers shower from the beyond. I am not telling you anything about Buddha, Christ, Krishna, Mahavira, Zarathustra, Mohammed, for a certain reason: because what they create is so subtle that you will not be able to catch hold of it. What Michelangelo creates is gross; what Van Gogh creates can be seen, is visible. What a Buddha creates is absolutely invisible. It needs a totally different kind of receptivity to understand. To understand a Buddha you have to be intelligent. Not only that Buddha's creation is of tremendous intelligence, but it is so superb, it is so supramental, that even to understand it you will have to be intelligent. Intellect won't help even in understanding.

Only two kinds of people create—the poets and the mystics. The poets create in the gross world and the mystics create in the subtle world. The poets create in the outer world—a painting, a poem, a song, music, a dance—and the mystic creates in the inner world. The poet's creativity is objective and the mystic's creativity is subjective, totally

> Creativity means bringing the new into existence, making a way for the unknown to penetrate the known, making a way for the sky to come to the earth. When there is a Beethoven or a Michelangelo or a Kalidas, the skies open, flowers shower from the beyond.

of the interior. First you have to understand the poet, only then can you understand one day—at least hope to understand one day—the mystic. The mystic is the highest flower of creativity. But you may not see anything that the mystic is doing.

Buddha has never painted a single picture, has never taken the brush in his hands, has not composed a single poem, has not sung a single song. Nobody has ever seen him dancing. If you watch him he is just sitting silently; his whole being is silence. Yes, a grace surrounds him, a grace of infinite beauty, of exquisite beauty, but you will need to be very vulnerable to feel it. You will have to be very open, not argumentative. You cannot be a spectator with a Buddha; you have to be a participant, because it is a mystery to be participated in. Then you will see what he is creating. He is creating consciousness, and consciousness is the purest form, the highest form possible, of expression.

A song is beautiful, a dance is beautiful because something of the divine is present in it. But in a Buddha the whole of God is present. That's why we have called Buddha "Bhagwan," we have called Mahavira "Bhagwan"—the whole of God is present.

Intellectual activity can make you experts in certain things, useful, efficient. But intellect is groping in the dark. It has no eyes, because it is not yet meditative. Intellect is borrowed, it has no insight of its own.

The subject was lovemaking. For weeks Arthur had successfully answered all the questions asked him on the television quiz show. He was now eligible for the jackpot prize of one hundred thousand dollars. For this one question he was allowed to call an expert. Arthur of course chose a world-famous professor of sexology from France.

The jackpot question was, "If you had been king during the first fifty years of the Assyrian empire, which three parts of your bride's anatomy would you have been expected to kiss on your wedding night?"

The first two answers came quickly. Arthur replied, "Her lips and her neck."

Now, stumped for the answer to the third part of the question, Arthur turned frantically to his expert. The Frenchman threw up his hands and groaned, "*Alors, mon ami*, do not ask me. I have been wrong twice already."

The expert, the knowledgeable, the intellectual, has no insight of his own. He depends on borrowed knowledge, on tradition, on convention. He carries libraries in his head, a great burden, but he has no vision. He knows much without knowing anything at all.

And because life is not the same, ever—it is constantly changing, moment to moment it is new—the expert always lags behind, his response is always inadequate. He can only react, he cannot respond, because he is not spontaneous. He has already arrived to conclusions. He is carrying ready-made answers—and the questions that life raises are always new.

Moreover, life is not a logical phenomenon, and the intellectual lives through logic; hence he never fits with life, and life never fits with him. Of course life is not at a loss, the intellectual himself is at a loss. He is always feeling like an outsider—not that life has expelled him; he himself has decided to remain outside life. If you cling too much to logic you will never be able to be part of the living process that this existence is.

Life is more than logic. Life is paradox, life is mystery.

> If you cling too much to logic you will never be able to be part of the living process that this existence is. Life is more than logic: life is paradox, life is mystery.

Gannaway and O'Casey arranged to fight a duel with pistols. Gannaway was quite fat, and when he saw his lean adversary facing him he objected.

"Debar!" he said, "I am twice as large as he is, so I ought to stand twice as far away from him as he is from me."

Absolutely logical, but how can you do it?

"Be easy now," replied his second. "I will soon put that right." And taking a piece of chalk from his pocket he drew two lines down the fat man's coat, leaving a space between them.

"Now," he said, turning to O'Casey, "fire away, and

remember that any hits outside that chalk line don't count."

Perfectly mathematical, perfectly logical!—but life is not so logical, life is not so mathematical. And people go on living in their intellects very logically. Logic gives them a feeling as if they know— but it is a big "as if" and one tends to forget it completely. Whatsoever you go on doing through intellect, it is only inference. It is not an experience of truth, but just an inference based on your logic—and your logic is your invention.

Cudahy, grogged to the gills, stood watching the Saint Patrick's Day parade. Unconsciously he dropped his lit cigarette into an old mattress that was lying at the curb.

Just then the gray-haired members of the Women's Nursing Corps came strutting by. At the same time, the smoldering mattress began giving off a dreadful smell.

Cudahy sniffed a couple of times and declared to a nearby cop, "Officer, they are marching those nurses too fast!"

Intellect may arrive at certain inferences, but intellect is an unconscious phenomenon. You are almost behaving sleepily.

Intelligence is awakening, and unless you are fully awake, whatsoever you decide is bound to be wrong somewhere or other. It is bound to be so, it is doomed to be wrong because it is a conclusion arrived at by an unconscious mind.

To bring intelligence into activity you don't need more information, you need more meditation. You need to become more silent, you need to become more thoughtless. You need to become less mind and more heart. You need to become aware of the magic that surrounds you—magic that is life, magic that is God, magic that is in the green trees and the red flowers, magic that is in people's eyes. Magic is happening everywhere! All is miraculous, but because of your intellect you remain closed inside yourself, clinging to your stupid conclusions arrived at in unconsciousness or given to you by others who are as unconscious as you are.

But intelligence is certainly creative, because intelligence brings your totality into functioning—not only a part, a small part, the head. Intelligence vibrates your whole being; each cell of your being, each fiber of your life starts dancing and falls into a subtle harmony with the total.

That's what creativity is: to pulsate in absolute harmony with the total. Things will start happening on their own. Your heart will start pouring songs of joy, your hands will start transforming things. You will touch mud and it will become a lotus. You will be able to become an alchemist. But it is possible only through great awakening of intelligence, great awakening of the heart.

> Intellect may arrive at certain inferences, but intellect is an unconscious phenomenon. You are almost behaving sleepily. Intelligence is awakening, and unless you are fully awake, whatsoever you decide is bound to be wrong somewhere or other.

4. BELIEF

A creator will not carry many beliefs—in fact, none. He will carry

> To bring intelligence into activity you don't need more information, you need more meditation. You need to become more silent, you need to become more thoughtless. You need to become less mind and more heart.

only his own experiences. And the beauty of experience is that the experience is always open, because further exploration is possible. Belief is always closed; it comes to a full point. Belief is always finished. Experience is never finished, it remains unfinished. While you are living, how can your experience be finished? Your experience is growing, it is changing, it is moving. It is continuously moving from the known into the unknown and from the unknown into the unknowable. And remember, experience has a beauty because it is unfinished. Some of the greatest songs are those which are unfinished. Some of the greatest books are those which are unfinished. Some of the greatest art is that which is unfinished. The unfinished has a beauty.

I have heard a Zen parable:

A king went to a Zen master to learn gardening. The master taught him for three years—and the king had a beautiful, big garden—thousands of gardeners were employed there—and whatsoever the master would say, the king would go and experiment in his garden. After three years the garden was absolutely ready, and the king invited the master to come and see the garden. The king was very nervous too, because the master was strict: "Will he appreciate?"—this was going to be a kind of examination—"Will he say, 'Yes, you have understood me'?"

Every care was taken. The garden was so beautifully complete, nothing was missing. Only then did the king bring the master to see. But the master was sad from the very beginning. He looked around, he moved in the garden from this side to that, he became more and more serious. The king became very frightened. He had never seen him so serious: "Why does he look so sad? Is there something so wrong?"

And again and again the master was shaking his head, and saying to himself, "No."

The king asked, "What is the matter, sir? What is wrong? Why don't you tell me? You are becoming so serious and sad, and you shake your head. Why? What is wrong? I don't see anything wrong, this is what you have been telling me and I have practiced it in this garden."

The master said, "It is so finished that it is dead. It is so complete—that's why I am shaking my head and I am saying no. Where are the dead leaves? Where are the dry leaves? I don't see a single dry leaf!" All the dry leaves were removed—on the paths there were no dry leaves; in the trees there were no dry leaves, no old leaves that had become yellow. "Where are those leaves?"

The king said, "I have told my gardeners to remove everything, to make it as absolute perfect as possible."

And the master said, "That's why it looks so dull, so manmade. God's things are never finished." And the master rushed out, outside the garden where all the dry leaves were heaped up. He brought a few dry leaves in a bucket, threw them to the winds, and the wind took them and started playing with the dry leaves and they started moving on the paths. He was delighted. He said, "Look, how alive it looks!" And sound had entered with the dry leaves— the music of the dry leaves, the wind playing with them. Now the garden had a whisper; otherwise it was dull and dead like a cemetery. That silence was not alive.

I love this story. The master said, "It is so complete, that's why it is wrong."

Just the other night a woman was here. She was telling me that she is writing a novel, and she is very puzzled about what to do. It has come to a point where it can be finished, but the possibility is that it can be lengthened; it is not yet complete. I told her, "You finish it. Finish it while it is unfinished—then it has something mysterious around it—that unfinishedness. . . . And I told her, "If your main character still wants to do something, let him become a sannyasin, a seeker. And then things are beyond your capacity. Then what can you do? Then it comes to a finish and yet things go on growing."

No story can be beautiful if it is utterly finished. It will be utterly dead. Experience always remains open—that means unfinished. Belief is always complete and finished. The first quality is an openness to experience.

Mind is all your beliefs collected together. Openness means no-mind; openness means you put your mind aside and you are ready to look into life again and again in a new way, not with the old eyes. The mind gives you the old eyes, it gives you again ideas: "Look through this." But then the thing becomes colored; then you don't look at it, then you project an idea upon it. Then the truth becomes a screen on which you go on projecting.

Look through no-mind, look through nothingness, *shunyata*. When you look through no-mind, your perception is efficient, because then you see that which is. And truth liberates. Everything else creates a bondage, only truth liberates.

In those moments of no-mind, truth starts filtering into you like light. The more you enjoy this light, this truth, the more you become capable and courageous to drop your mind. Sooner or later a day comes when you look and you don't have any mind. You are not looking for anything, you are simply looking. Your look is pure. In that moment you become *avalokita*, one who looks with pure eyes. That is one of the names of Buddha—'Avalokita.' He looks with no ideas, he simply looks.

CREATIVITY HAS NOTHING TO DO WITH ANY ACTIVITY IN PARTICULAR, with painting, poetry, dancing, singing—it has nothing to do with anything in particular. Anything can be creative, it is you who brings that quality to the activity. Activity itself is neither creative nor uncreative. You can paint in an uncreative way, you can sing in an uncreative way. You can clean the floor in a creative way, you can cook in a creative way. Creativity is the quality that you bring to the activity you are doing. It is an attitude, an inner approach— how you look at things.

So the first thing to be remembered is, don't confine creativity to anything in particular. It is the person who is creative—and if a man is creative then whatsoever he does . . . even if he walks you can see in his walking there is creativity. Even if he sits silently and does nothing—even nondoing will be a creative act. Bud-

> Mind is all your beliefs collected together. Openness means no-mind, openness means you put your mind aside and you are ready to look into life again and again in a new way, not with the old eyes.

dha sitting under the bodhi tree doing nothing is the greatest creator the world has ever known.

Once you understand it—that it is you, the person, who is creative or uncreative—then the problem of feeling like you are uncreative disappears.

Not everybody can be a painter—and there is no need either. If everybody is a painter the world will be very ugly; it will be difficult to live! Not everybody can be a dancer, and there is no need. But everybody can be creative.

> ☙
>
> Creativity is the quality that you bring to the activity you are doing. It is an attitude, an inner approach—how you look at things.

Whatsoever you do, if you do it joyfully, if you do it lovingly, if your act of doing it is not purely economic, then it is creative. If something grows out of it within you, if it gives you growth, it is spiritual, it is creative, it is divine. You become more divine as you become more creative. All the religions of the world have said God is the creator. I don't know whether he is the creator or not, but one thing I know: the more creative you become, the more godly you become. When your creativity comes to a climax, when your whole life becomes creative, you live in God. So he must be the creator because people who have been creative have been closest to him.

Love what you do. Be meditative while you are doing it— whatsoever it is, irrespective of the fact of what it is. Then you will know that even cleaning can become creative. With what love!— almost singing and dancing inside. If you clean the floor with such love, you have done an invisible painting. You lived that moment in such delight that it has given you some inner growth. You cannot be the same after a creative act.

Creativity means loving whatsoever you do—enjoying, celebrating it! Maybe nobody comes to know about it—who is going to praise you for cleaning the floor? History will not take any account of it, newspapers will not publish your name and picture, but that is irrelevant. You enjoyed it. The value is intrinsic.

So if you are looking for fame and then you think you are creative—if you become famous like Picasso, then you are creative—then you will miss. Then you are in fact not creative at all; you are a politician, ambitious. If fame happens, good. If it doesn't happen, good. It should not be the consideration. The consideration should be that you are enjoying whatsoever you are doing, it is your love affair.

If your act is your love affair, then it becomes creative. Small things become great by the touch of love and delight.

> Whatsoever you do, if you do it joyfully, if you do it lovingly, if your act of doing it is not purely economic, then it is creative.

But if you believe you are uncreative, you will become uncreative—because belief is not just belief. It opens doors and it closes doors. If you have a wrong belief, then that will hang around you as a closed door. If you believe that you are uncreative, you will become uncreative because that belief will obstruct, continuously negate, all possibilities of flowing. It will not allow your energy to flow because you will continually be saying, "I am uncreative."

This has been taught to everybody. Very few people are accepted as creative—a few painters, a few poets, one in a million. This is foolish! Every human being is a born creator. Watch children and you will see: all children are creative. By and by, we destroy their creativity. By and by, we force wrong beliefs on them. By and by, we distract them. By and by, we make them more and more economical and political and ambitious.

When ambition enters, creativity disappears—because an ambitious man cannot be creative, an ambitious man cannot love any activity for its own sake. While he is painting he is looking ahead; he is thinking, "When am I going to get a Nobel prize?" When he is writing a novel he is looking ahead, he is always in the future—and a creative person is always in the present.

We destroy creativity. Nobody is born uncreative, but we make ninety-nine percent of people uncreative. But just throwing the responsibility on the society is not going to help. You have to take your life in your own hands. You have to drop wrong conditionings. You have to drop wrong, hypnotic suggestions that have been given to you in your childhood. Drop them! Purify yourself of all conditionings . . . and suddenly you will see you are creative.

To be and to be creative are synonymous. It is impossible to

> If fame happens, good. If it doesn't happen, good. It should not be the consideration. The consideration should be that you are enjoying whatsoever you are doing. It is your love affair.

be and not to be creative. But that impossible thing has happened, that ugly phenomenon has happened because all your creative sources have been plugged, blocked, destroyed, and your whole energy has been forced into some activity that the society thinks is going to pay.

Our whole attitude about life is money oriented. And money is one of the most uncreative things one can become interested in. Our whole approach is power oriented and power is destructive, not creative. A man who is after money will become destructive because money has to be robbed, exploited; it has to be taken away from many people, only then can you have it. Power simply means you have to make many people impotent; you have to destroy them; only then will you be powerful, can you be powerful. Remember, these are destructive acts.

A creative act enhances the beauty of the world; it gives something to the world, it never takes anything from it. A creative person comes into the world, enhances the beauty of the world—a song here, a painting there. He makes the world dance better, enjoy better, love better, meditate better. When he leaves this world, he leaves a better world behind him. Nobody may know him, some-

> Belief is not just belief. It opens doors, it closes doors. If you have a wrong belief, then that will hang around you as a closed door. If you believe that you are uncreative, you will become uncreative because that belief will obstruct, continuously negate, all possibilities of flowing.

> ❧
>
> Very few people are accepted as creative—a few painters, a few poets, one in a million. This is foolish! Every human being is a born creator. Watch children and you will see: all children are creative.

body may know him, that is not the point—but he leaves the world a better world, tremendously fulfilled because his life has been of some intrinsic value.

Money, power, prestige, are uncreative—not only uncreative but destructive activities. Beware of them! And if you beware of them you can become creative very easily. I am not saying that your creativity is going to give you power, prestige, money. No, I cannot promise you any rose gardens. It may give you trouble. It may force you to live a poor man's life. All that I can promise you is that deep inside you will be the richest man possible; deep inside you will be fulfilled, deep inside you will be full of joy and celebration. You will be continuously receiving more and more blessings, your life will be a life of benediction.

It is possible that outwardly you may not be famous, you may not have money, you may not succeed in the so-called world. But to succeed in this so-called world is to fail deeply, is to fail in the inside world. And what are you going to do with the whole world at your feet if you have lost your own self? What will you do if you possess the whole world and you don't possess yourself? A creative person possesses his own being; he is a master.

That's why in the East we have been calling seekers "swamis."

Swami means a master. Beggars have been called swamis—masters. Emperors we have known but they proved in the final account, in the final conclusion of their lives, that they were beggars. A man who is after money and power and prestige is a beggar because he continuously begs, he has nothing to give to the world.

Be a giver. Share whatsoever you can—and remember, I am not making any distinction between small things and great things. If you can smile wholeheartedly, hold somebody's hand and smile, then it is a creative act, a great creative act. Just embrace somebody to your heart and you are creative. Just look with loving eyes at somebody . . . just a loving look can change the whole world of a person.

Be creative. Don't be worried about what you are doing—one has to do many things—but do everything creatively, with devotion. Then your work becomes worship, then whatsoever you do is a prayer and whatsoever you do is an offering at the altar.

Drop all beliefs that you are uncreative. I know how these beliefs are created—you may not have been a gold medalist in the university, you may not have been top

> If you can smile wholeheartedly, hold somebody's hand and smile, then it is a creative act, a great creative act. Just embrace somebody to your heart and you are creative. Just look with loving eyes at somebody . . . just a loving look can change the whole world of a person.

in your class. Your painting may not have won appreciation; when you play on your flute, neighbors report to the police! But just because of these things, don't get the wrong belief that you are uncreative.

It may be because you are imitating others. People have a very limited idea of what being creative is—playing the guitar or the flute, or writing poetry—so people go on writing rubbish in the name of poetry. You have to find out what you can do and what you cannot do. Everybody cannot do everything! You have to search and find your destiny. You have to grope in the dark, I know. It is not very clear-cut what your destiny is—but that's how life is. And it is good that one has to search for it; in the very search, something grows.

If a chart of your life were to be given to you when you were entering into the world—"This will be your life, you are going to become a guitarist"—then your life would be mechanical. Only a machine can be predicted, not a man. Man is unpredictable. Man is always an opening . . . a potentiality for a thousand and one things. Many doors open and many alternatives are always present at each step—and you have to choose, you have to feel. But if you love your life, you will be able to find.

If you don't love your life and you love something else, then there is a problem. If you love money and you want to be creative, you cannot become creative. The very ambition for money is going to destroy your creativity. If you want fame, then forget about creativity. Fame comes easier if you are destructive. Fame comes easier to an Adolf Hitler, fame comes easier to a Henry Ford. Fame is easier if you are competitive, violently competitive. If you can kill and destroy people, fame comes easier.

The whole of history is the history of murderers. If you become a murderer, fame will be very easy. You can become a prime minister, you can become a president—but these are all masks. Behind them you will find very violent people, terribly violent people hiding, smiling. Those smiles are political, diplomatic. If the mask slips, you will always see Genghis Khan, Tamerlane, Nadir Shah, Napoleon, Alexander, Hitler, hiding behind.

If you want fame, don't talk about creativity. I am not saying that fame never comes to a creative person—but very rarely it comes, very rarely. It is more like an accident, and it takes much time. Almost always it happens that by the time fame comes to a creative person, he is gone—it is always posthumous, it is delayed.

Jesus was not famous in his day. If there were no Bible, there would have been no record of him. The record belongs to his four disciples; nobody else has ever mentioned him, whether he existed or not. He was not famous. He was not successful—can you think of a greater failure than Jesus? But, by and by, he became more and more significant; by and by, people recognized him. It takes time.

The greater a person is the more time it takes for people to recognize him—because when a great person is born, there are no criteria to judge him by, there are no maps to find him with. He has to create his own values; by the time he has created

If you really want to be creative, then there is no question of money, success, prestige, respectability—then you enjoy your activity, then each act has an intrinsic value. You dance because you like dancing, you dance because you delight in it.

those values he is gone. It takes hundreds of years for a creative person to be recognized, and then too it is not certain. There have been many creative people who have never been recognized. It is accidental for a creative person to be successful. For an uncreative, destructive person it is more certain.

So if you are seeking something else in the name of creativity, then drop the idea of being creative. At least consciously, deliberately, do whatsoever you want to do. Never hide behind masks. If you really want to be creative, then there is no question of money, success, prestige, respectability—then you enjoy your activity, then each act has an intrinsic value. You dance because you like dancing; you dance because you delight in it. If somebody appreciates, good, you feel grateful. If nobody appreciates, it is none of your business to be worried about it. You danced, you enjoyed—you are already fulfilled.

But any belief of being uncreative can be dangerous—drop it! Nobody is uncreative—not even trees, not even rocks. People who have known trees and loved trees know that each tree creates its own space. Each rock creates its own space, it is like nobody else's space. If you become sensitive, if you become capable of under-standing, through empathy, you will be tremendously benefited. You will see that each tree is creative in its own way; no other tree is like it—each tree is unique, each tree has individuality. Each rock has individuality. Trees are not just trees, they are people. Rocks are not just rocks, they are people. Go and sit by the side of a rock—watch it lovingly, touch it lovingly, feel it lovingly.

It is said about a Zen master that he was able to pull very big rocks, remove very big rocks—and he was a very fragile man. It was almost impossible looking at his physiology—stronger men, very much stronger than him, were unable to pull those rocks, and he would simply pull them very easily.

He was asked what his trick was. He said, "There is no trick—I love the rock, so the rock helps. First I say to her, 'Now my prestige is in your hands, and these people have come to watch. Now help me, cooperate with me.' Mm? Then I simply hold the rock lovingly . . . and wait for the hint. When the rock gives me the hint—it is a shudder, my whole spine starts vibrating—when the rock gives me the hint that she is ready, then I move. You move against the rock, that's why so much energy is needed. I move with the rock, I flow with the rock. In fact, it is wrong to say that I move it—I am simply there. The rock moves itself."

One great Zen master was a carpenter, and whenever he made tables, chairs, somehow they had some ineffable quality in them, a tremendous magnetism. He was asked, "How do you make them?"

He said, "I don't make them. I simply go to the forest . . . the basic thing is to inquire of the forest, of trees, which tree is ready to become a chair."

Now these things look absurd because we don't know, we don't know the language. For three days he would remain in the forest. He would sit under one tree, under another tree, and he would talk to trees—he was a madman! But a tree is to be judged by its fruit, and this master has also to be judged by his creation. A few of his chairs still survive in China—they still carry a magnetism. You will just be simply attracted. You will not know what is pulling you—after a thousand years! Something tremendously beautiful.

He said, "I go and I say that I am in search of a tree who wants to become a chair. I ask the trees if they are willing—not only willing but cooperating with me, ready to go with me—only then. Sometimes it happens that no tree is ready to become a chair and I come back empty-handed."

> ≋
>
> Each person comes
> into this world with a
> specific destiny—he
> has something to
> fulfill, some message
> has to be delivered,
> some work has to be
> completed. You are
> not here accidentally—
> you are here
> meaningfully. The
> whole intends to do
> something through
> you.

It happened: The emperor of China asked him to make him a stand for his books. And he went to the forest and after three days he said, "Wait—no tree is ready to come to the palace."

After three months the emperor again inquired. The carpenter said, "I have been going continually. I am persuading. Wait—one tree seems to be leaning a little bit."

Finally he persuaded one tree. He said, "The whole art is there! When the tree comes of its own accord then she is simply asking the help of the carpenter."

If you are loving you will see that the whole existence has individuality. Don't pull and push things. Watch, communicate, take their help—and much energy will be preserved.

Even trees are creative, rocks are creative. You are human, the very culmination of this existence. You are at the top—you are conscious. Never think with wrong beliefs and never be attached to wrong beliefs that you are uncreative. Maybe your father said to you that you are uncreative, your colleagues said to you that you are uncreative. Maybe you were searching in wrong directions, in directions where you are not creative. But there must be a direction in which you are creative. Seek and search and remain available, and go on groping until you find it.

Each person comes into this world with a specific destiny—he has something to fulfill, some message has to be delivered, some work has to be completed. You are not here accidentally—you are here meaningfully. There is a purpose behind you. The whole intends to do something through you.

5. THE FAME GAME

Our whole life's structure is such that we are taught that unless there is a recognition we are nobody, we are worthless. The work is not important, but the recognition is—and this is putting things upside down. The work should be important, a joy in itself. You should work not to be recognized, but because you enjoy being creative; you love the work for its own sake.

This should be the way to look at things—you work if you love it, don't ask for recognition. If it comes, take it easily; if it does not come, don't think about it. Your fulfillment should be in the work itself. And if everybody learns this simple art of loving his work, whatever it is, enjoying it without asking for any recognition, we would have a more beautiful and celebrating world.

As it is, the world has trapped you in a miserable pattern. What you are doing is not good because you love it, because you do it perfectly, but because the world recognizes it, rewards it, gives you gold medals, Nobel prizes. They have taken away the whole intrinsic value of creativity and destroyed millions of people—because you cannot give millions of people Nobel prizes. But you have created the desire for recognition in everybody, so nobody can work peacefully, silently, enjoying whatever he is doing. And life consists of small things. For those small things there are no rewards, no titles given by the governments, no honorary degrees given by the universities.

One of the great poets of this century, Rabindranath Tagore, lived in Bengal, India. He had published his poetry, his novels, in Bengali—but no recognition came to him. Then he translated a small book, *Gitanjali*, "Offering of Songs," into English. He was aware that the original has a beauty that the translation does not have and cannot have—because these two languages, Bengali and English, have different structures, different ways of expression. Bengali is very sweet. Even if you fight, it seems you are engaged in a nice conversation. It is very musical, each word is musical. That quality is not in English and cannot be brought to it; English has different qualities. But somehow he managed to translate it, and the translation—which is a poor thing compared to the original—received the Nobel prize. Then suddenly the whole of India became aware . . . The book had been available in Bengali and in other Indian languages, for years and nobody had taken any note of it.

Every university wanted to give him a DLitt. Calcutta, where he lived, was the first university, obviously, to offer him an honorary degree. He refused. He said, "You are not giving a degree to me; you are not giving a recognition to my work, you are giving recognition to the Nobel prize—because the book has been here in a far more beautiful way, and nobody has bothered even to write a review of it." He refused to take any honorary degrees. He said, "It is insulting to me."

Jean-Paul Sartre, one of the great novelists and a man of tremendous insight into human psychology, refused the Nobel prize. He said, "I have received enough reward while I was creating my work. A Nobel prize cannot add anything to it—on the contrary, it pulls me down. It is good for amateurs who are in search of recognition; I am old enough and I have enjoyed enough. I have loved whatever I have done, it was its own reward. And I don't want any other reward, because nothing can be better than that which I have already received." And he was right. But the right people are so few in the world, and the world is full of wrong people living in traps.

Why should you bother about recognition? Bothering about recognition has meaning only if you don't love your work; then it is meaningful, then it seems to substitute. You hate the work, you don't like it, but you are doing it because there will be recognition, you will be appreciated, accepted. Rather than thinking about recognition, reconsider your work. Do you love it? Then that is the end. If you don't love it, then change it!

The parents, the teachers are always reinforcing that you should be recognized, you should be accepted. This is a very cunning strategy to keep people under control.

Learn one basic thing: do whatever you want to do, love to do. And never ask for recognition, that is begging. Why should one ask for recognition? Why should one hanker for acceptance? Deep down in yourself, look. Perhaps you don't like what you are doing, perhaps you are afraid that you are on the wrong track, so acceptance will help you

> Bothering about recognition has meaning only if you don't love your work, then it is meaningful, then it seems to substitute. You hate the work, you don't like it, but you are doing it because there will be recognition, you will be appreciated, accepted.

feel that you are right. Recognition will make you feel that you are going toward the right goal.

The question is of your own inner feelings; it has nothing to do with the outside world. And why depend on others? All these things depend on others—you yourself are becoming dependent. I will not accept any Nobel prize. All the condemnation I have received from all the nations around the world, from all the religions, is more valuable to me! Accepting the Nobel prize means I am becoming dependent—now I will not be proud of myself but proud of the Nobel prize. Right now I can only be proud of myself; there is nothing else I can be proud of.

In this way you become an individual. And to be an individual living in total freedom, on your own feet, drinking from your own sources, is what makes a man really centered, rooted. That is the beginning of his ultimate flowering.

These so-called recognized people, honored people, are full of rubbish and nothing else. But they are full of the rubbish that the society wants them to be filled with—and the society compensates them by giving them rewards.

> Any man who has any sense of his own individuality lives by his own love, by his own work, without caring at all what others think of it.

Any man who has any sense of his own individuality lives by his own love, by his own work, without caring at all what others think of it. The more valuable your work is, the less is the possibility of getting any respectability for it. And if your work is the work of a genius, then you are not going to see any respect in your lifetime. You will be condemned in your lifetime . . . then, after two or three centuries, statues of you will be made, your books will be respected—because it takes almost two or three centuries for humanity to pick up as much intelligence as a genius has today. The gap is vast.

Being respected by idiots you have to behave according to their manners, their expectations. To be respected by this sick humanity you have to be sicker than they are. Then they will respect you. But what will you gain? You will lose your soul and you will gain nothing.

FOUR KEYS

Whenever you are creating, you will have the taste of life—and it will depend on your intensity, on your totality. Life is not a philosophical problem, it is a religious mystery. Then anything can become the door—even cleaning the floor. If you can do it creatively, lovingly, totally, you will have some taste of life.

1. BECOME A CHILD AGAIN

Become a child again and you will be creative. All children are creative. Creativity needs freedom—freedom from the mind, freedom from knowledge, freedom from prejudices. A creative person is one who can try the new. A creative person is not a robot. Robots are never creative, they are repetitive.

So become a child again—and you will be surprised that all children are creative. All children, wherever they are born, are creative—but we don't allow their creativity. We crush and kill their creativity, we jump upon them; we start teaching them the right way to do things.

Remember, a creative person always goes on trying the wrong

ways. If you always follow the right way to do a thing you will never be creative, because the "right way" means the way discovered by others. And the right way means that of course you will be able to make something, you will become a producer, a manufacturer, you will be a technician, but you will not be a creator.

What is the difference between a producer and a creator? A producer knows the right way of doing a thing, the most economical way of doing a thing; with the least effort he can create more results. He is a producer. A creator fools around. He does not know what is the right way to do a thing so he goes on seeking and searching again and again in different directions. Many times he moves in a wrong direction—but wherever he moves, he learns; he becomes more and more rich. He does something that nobody has ever done before. If he had followed the right way to do things he would not have been able to do it.

> Remember, a creative person always goes on trying the wrong ways. If you always follow the right way to do a thing you will never be creative—because the right way means the way discovered by others.

Listen to this small story:

A Sunday school teacher asked her students to draw a picture of the holy family. After the pictures were brought to her, she saw that some of the youngsters had drawn the conventional pictures—the holy family in the manger, the holy family riding on the mule, and the like.

But she called up one little boy to ask him to explain his drawing, which showed an airplane with four heads sticking out of the plane windows.

She said, "I can understand why you drew three of the heads to show Joseph, Mary, and Jesus. But who's the fourth head?"

"Oh," answered the boy, "that's Pontius the Pilot!"

Now this is beautiful! This is what creativity is, he has discovered something. But only children can do that. You will be afraid to do it, afraid you will look foolish.

A creator has to be able to look foolish. A creator has to risk his so-called respectability. That's why you always see that poets, painters, dancers, musicians are not very respectable people. And when they become respectable, when a Nobel prize is given to them, they are no longer creative. From that moment creativity disappears.

> A creator has to be able to look foolish. A creator has to risk his so-called respectability. That's why you always see that poets, painters, dancers, musicians, are not very respectable people.

What happens? Have you ever seen a Nobel prize winner writing another thing that is of any value? Have you ever seen any respectable person doing something creative? He becomes afraid. If he does something wrong, or if something goes wrong, what will happen to his prestige? He cannot afford that. So when an artist becomes respectable he becomes dead.

Only those who are ready to put their prestige, their pride, their respectability at stake again and again, and can go on into something that nobody thinks is worth going into . . . Creators are always thought to be mad people. The world recognizes them, but very late. It goes on thinking that something is wrong. Creators are eccentric people.

And remember again, each child is born with all the capacities to become a creator. Without any exception all children try to be creators, but we don't allow them. Immediately we start teaching them the right way to do a thing—and once they have learned the right way to do a thing they become robots. Then they go on doing the right thing again and again and again, and the more they do it the more efficient they become. And the more efficient they become, the more respected they are.

Somewhere between the age of seven and fourteen a great change happens in a child. Psychologists have been searching into the phenomenon . . . why does it happen and what happens?

You have two minds, two hemispheres in the brain. The left hemisphere of the mind is uncreative—it is technically very capable but as far as creativity is concerned it is absolutely impotent. It can do a thing only once it has learned it—and it can do it very efficiently, perfectly; it is mechanical. This left hemisphere is the hemisphere of reasoning, logic, mathematics. It is the hemisphere of calculation, cleverness, of discipline, order.

The right hemisphere is just the opposite of it. It is the hemisphere of chaos, not of order; it is the hemisphere of poetry, not of prose; it is the hemisphere of love, not of logic. It has a great feeling for beauty, it has a great insight into originality—but it is not efficient, it cannot be efficient. The creator cannot be efficient, he has to go on experimenting.

The creator cannot settle anywhere. The creator is a vagabond, he carries his tent on his shoulders. Yes, he can stay for an overnight visit, but by the morning he is gone again—that's why I call him a vagabond. He is never a householder. He cannot settle; settling means death to him. He is always ready to take a risk. Risk is his love affair.

But this is the right-side hemisphere. The right-side hemisphere is functioning when the child is born; the left-side hemisphere is not functioning. Then we start teaching the child—unknowingly, unscientifically. Down the ages we have learned the trick of how to shift the energy from the right hemisphere to the left hemisphere. How to put a stop to the right hemisphere and how to start the left hemisphere—that's what our whole schooling is. From kindergarten to university that's what our whole training and so-called education are—an effort to destroy the right hemisphere and to help the left hemisphere. Somewhere between the ages of seven and fourteen we succeed and the child is killed, the child is destroyed.

Then the child is wild no more—he becomes a citizen. Then he learns the ways of discipline, language, logic, prose. He starts competing in the school, becomes an egoist, starts learning all the neurotic things that are prevalent in the society. He becomes more interested in power, money, starts thinking how to become more educated so that he can become more powerful. How to have more money, how to have a big house, and all that . . . he shifts. Then the right hemisphere functions less and less—or functions only when you are in dream, fast asleep. Or sometimes when you have taken a drug. . . .

The great appeal of drugs in the West is only because the West has succeeded in destroying the right hemisphere completely because of compulsory education. The West has become too educated—that means it has gone to the very extreme, to one side. Now there seems to be no possibility . . . Unless you introduce some means that can help the right hemisphere to be revived again in the universities and colleges and the schools, drugs are not going to go. There is no possibility of prohibiting drugs by law alone. There is no way to enforce it unless the inner balance is put right again.

The appeal of the drug is that it immediately shifts gear—from the left hemisphere your energy moves to the right hemisphere. That's all the drug can do. Alcohol has been doing it for centuries, but now far better drugs are available—LSD, marijuana, psilocybin, and even better drugs will be available in the future.

And the criminal is not the drug taker, the criminal is the politician and the educationist. It is they who are guilty. They have forced the human mind into one extreme—into such an extreme that now there is a need to revolt. And the need is so great! Poetry has completely disappeared from people's lives, beauty has disappeared, love has disappeared—money, power, influence, they have become the only gods.

How can humanity go on living without love and without poetry and without joy and without celebration? Not for long. And the new generation all over the world is doing a great service by showing the stupidity of your so-called education. It is not a coincidence that drug takers almost always become dropouts. They disappear from the universities, colleges. It is not a coincidence, this is part of the same revolt.

And once a man has learned the joys of drugs it becomes very difficult for him to drop them. Drugs can be dropped only if better ways can be found that can release your poetry. Meditation is a better way—less destructive, less harmful than any kind of chemical. In fact it is not harmful at all; it is beneficial. Meditation also does the same thing: it shifts your mind from the left hemisphere to the right hemisphere. It releases your inner capacity of creativity.

A great calamity that is going to arise in the world through drugs can be avoided by only one thing—that is meditation. There is no other way. If meditation becomes more and more prevalent and enters people's lives more and more, drugs will disappear.

And education must start to be not so absolutely against the right hemisphere and its functioning. If the children are taught that both sides exist in their minds, and if they are taught how to use both and when to use which . . . There are situations when only the left-side brain is needed, when you need to calculate—in the marketplace, in the everyday business of life—and there are times when you need the right hemisphere.

And remember always, the right hemisphere is the end and the left hemisphere is the means. The left hemisphere has to serve the right hemisphere. The right hemisphere is the master—because you earn money only because you want to enjoy your life and celebrate your life. You want a certain bank balance only so that you can love. You work only so that you can play—play remains the goal. You work only so that you can relax. Relaxation remains the goal, work is not the goal.

The work ethic is a hangover from the past; it has to be dropped. And the educational world has to go through a real revolution. People should not be forced, children should not be forced into repetitive patterns. What is your education? Have you ever looked into it? Have you ever pondered over it? It is simply a training in memory. You don't become intelligent through it, you become more and more unintelligent. You become stupid! Each child enters the school very intelligent but it is very rare that a person comes out of university and is still intelligent—it is very rare. The university almost always succeeds. Yes, you come with degrees, but you have purchased those degrees at a great cost: you have lost your intelligence, you have lost your joy, you have lost life—because you have lost the functioning of the right-side hemisphere.

And what have you learned? Information. Your mind is full of memory; you can repeat, you can reproduce. That's what your examinations are—a person is thought to be very intelligent if he can vomit all that has been thrown into him. First he has to be forced to swallow, go on swallowing, and then in the examination papers, vomit. If you can vomit efficiently, you are intelligent. If you can vomit exactly that which has been given to you, you are intelligent.

> ❧
>
> The work ethic is a hangover from the past. It has to be dropped. And the educational world has to go through a real revolution. Children should not be forced into repetitive patterns.

Now this is something to be understood: you can vomit the same thing only if you have not digested it, remember. If you have digested it you cannot vomit the same thing. Something else may come, blood may come, but not the same loaf of bread you have eaten—that will not come, it has disappeared. So you have to simply keep it down there in your stomach without digesting it—then you are thought to be very, very intelligent. The most stupid are thought to be the most intelligent. It is a very sorry state of things.

The intelligent may not fit. Do you know Albert Einstein could not pass his matriculation examination? Such a creative intelligence—it was difficult for him to behave in the stupid way that everybody else was behaving.

All your so-called gold medalists in the schools, colleges, universities disappear. They never prove to be of any use. Their glory ends with their gold medals, then they are never found anywhere; life owes nothing to them. What happens to these people? You have destroyed them. They have purchased the certificates and they have lost all. Now they will be carrying their certificates and degrees.

This kind of education has to be totally transformed. More joy has to be brought to the schoolroom, more chaos has to be brought to the university—more dance, more song, more poetry, more creativity, more intelligence. Such dependence on memory has to be dropped.

People should be watched, and people should be helped to be more intelligent. When a person responds in a new way he should be valued. There should be no right answer— there is none, there is only a stupid answer and an intelligent answer. The very categorization of right and

> ❧
>
> When a person responds in a new way he should be valued. There should be no right answer— there is none, there is only a stupid answer and an intelligent answer. The very categorization of right and wrong is wrong.

wrong is wrong; there is no right answer and there is no wrong answer. Either the answer is stupid, repetitive, or the answer is creative, responsive, intelligent. Even if the repetitive answer seems to be right it should not be valued much, because it is repetitive. And even though the intelligent answer may not be perfectly right, may not fit with the old ideas, it has to be praised because it is new. It shows intelligence.

If you want to be creative, what should you do? Undo all that the society has done to you. Undo all that your parents and your teachers have done to you. Undo all that the policeman and the politician and the priest have done to you—and you will again become creative, you will again have that thrill that you had in the very beginning. It is still waiting there, repressed. It can uncoil. And when that creative energy uncoils in you, you are religious. To me, a religious person is one who is a creative person. Everybody is born creative, but very few people remain creative.

It is for you to come out of the trap. You can. Of course, you will need great courage, because when you start undoing what the society has done to you, you will lose respect. You will not be thought to be respectable, you will look bizarre to people. You will look like a freak,

> If you want to be creative, what should you do? Undo all that the society has done to you. Undo all that your parents and your teachers have done to you. Undo all that the policeman and the politician and the priest have done to you—and you will again become creative.

people will think, "Something has gone wrong with the poor man." This is the greatest courage—to go into a life where people start thinking you are bizarre.

Naturally, you have to risk. If you want to be creative you will have to risk all. But it is worth it. A little creativity is more worthwhile than this whole world and its kingdom.

2. BE READY TO LEARN

Discipline is a beautiful word, but it has been misused as all other beautiful words have been misused in the past. The word *discipline* comes from the same root as the word *disciple*—the root meaning of the word is "a process of learning." One who is ready to learn is a disciple, and the process of being ready to learn is discipline.

The knowledgeable person is never ready to learn, because he already thinks he knows; he is very centered in his so-called knowledge. His knowledge is nothing but a nourishment for his ego. He cannot be a disciple, he cannot be in true discipline.

Socrates says: "I know only one thing, that I know nothing"—that is the beginning of discipline. When you don't know anything, of course, of course a great longing arises to inquire, explore, investigate. And the moment you start learning, another factor follows inevitably: whatsoever you have learned has to be dropped continuously; otherwise it will become knowledge, and knowledge will prevent further learning.

The real man of discipline never accumulates; each moment he dies to whatsoever he has come to know and again becomes ignorant. That ignorance is really luminous. I agree with Dionysius when he calls ignorance luminous. It is one of the most beautiful experiences in existence to be in a state of luminous not knowing. When you are in that state of not knowing you are open, there is no barrier, you are ready to explore.

Discipline has been misinterpreted. People have been telling others to discipline their life, to do this, not to do that. Thousands of shoulds and should nots have been imposed on man. And when a man lives with thousands of shoulds and should nots, he cannot be creative. He is a prisoner; everywhere he will come across a wall.

The creative person has to dissolve all shoulds and should nots. He needs freedom and space, vast space; he needs the whole sky and all the stars. Only then can his innermost spontaneity start growing.

So remember, my meaning of discipline is not that of any Ten Commandments; I am not giving you any discipline, I am simply giving you an insight into how to keep learning and never become knowledgeable. Your discipline has to come from your very heart, it has to be your own—and there is a great

> The real man of discipline never accumulates, each moment he dies to whatsoever he has come to know and again becomes ignorant. That ignorance is really luminous.

difference. When somebody else gives you the discipline, it can never fit you; it will be like wearing somebody else's clothes. Either they will be too loose or too tight, and you will always feel a little bit silly in them.

Mohammed has given a discipline to the Mohammedans; it may have been good for him, but it cannot be good for anybody

> The creative person has to dissolve all shoulds and should nots. He needs freedom and space, vast space, he needs the whole sky and all the stars, only then can his innermost spontaneity start growing.

else. Buddha has given a discipline to millions of Buddhists; it may have been good for him, but it cannot be good for anybody else. A discipline is an individual phenomenon; whenever you borrow it you start living according to set principles, dead principles. And life is never dead; life is constantly changing each moment. Life is a flux.

Heraclitus is right: you cannot step in the same river twice. In fact, I myself would like to say you cannot step in the same river even once, the river is moving so fast! One has to be alert to, watchful of, each situation and its nuances, and one has to respond to the situation according to the moment, not according to any ready-made answers given by others.

Do you see the stupidity of humanity? Five thousand years ago, Manu gave a discipline to the Hindus and they are still following it. Three thousand years ago Moses gave a discipline to the Jews and they are still following it. Five thousand years ago Adinatha gave his discipline to the Jains and they are still following it. The whole world is being driven crazy by these disciplines! They are out of date, they should have been buried long, long ago. You are carrying corpses, and those corpses are stinking. And when you live surrounded by corpses, what kind of life can you have?

I teach you the moment and the freedom of the moment and

the responsibility of the moment. One thing may be right this moment and may become wrong the next moment. Don't try to be consistent, otherwise you will be dead. Only dead people are consistent. Try to be alive, with all its inconsistencies, and live each moment without any reference to the past and without any reference to the future either. Live the moment in the context of the moment, and your response will be total. And that totality has beauty and that totality is creativity. Then whatsoever you do will have a beauty of its own.

3. FIND NIRVANA IN THE ORDINARY

Have you heard that a gardener who creates life, beautifies life, has received a Nobel prize? A farmer, who plows the field and brings nourishment to you all—has he ever been rewarded? No, he lives and dies as if he has never been here.

This is an ugly demarcation. Every creative soul—it does not matter what he creates—should be respected and honored, so that creativity is honored. But even politicians get Nobel prizes—who are nothing but clever criminals. All the bloodshed that has happened in the world has happened because of these politicians, and they are still preparing more and more nuclear weapons to commit a global suicide.

In a real, honest human society, creativity will be honored, respected, because the creative soul is participating in the work of God.

Our sense of aesthetics is not very rich.

I am reminded of Abraham Lincoln. He was the son of a shoemaker, and he became the president of America. Naturally, all the aristocrats were tremendously disturbed, annoyed, irritated. And it is not a coincidence that soon Abraham Lincoln was assassinated. They could not tolerate the idea that the country had a shoemaker's son as the president.

> Every creative soul—it does not matter what he creates—should be respected and honored, so that creativity is honored. But even politicians get Nobel prizes—who are nothing but clever criminals.

On the first day, when he was going to give his inaugural address to the Senate, just as he was going to stand up, one ugly aristocrat stood up and he said, "Mr. Lincoln, although by some accident you have become the president of the country, don't forget that you used to come with your father to my house to prepare shoes for our family. And there are many senators who are wearing the shoes made by your father, so never forget your origins."

He was thinking he was going to humiliate him. But you cannot humiliate a man like Abraham Lincoln. Only small people, suffering from inferiority, can be humiliated; the greatest of human beings are beyond humiliation.

Abraham Lincoln said something which should be remembered by everyone. He said, "I am very grateful to you for reminding me of my father just before I give my first address to the Senate. My father was so beautiful, and such a creative artist—there was no other man who could make such beautiful shoes. I know perfectly well that whatever I do, I will never be such a great president as he was a great creator. I cannot surpass him.

"But by the way, I want to remind all you aristocrats that if the shoes made by my father are pinching you, I have also learned the art with him. I am not a great shoemaker, but at least I can correct your shoes. You just inform me, I will come to your house."

There was great silence in the Senate, and the senators understood that it was impossible to humiliate this man. But he had shown a tremendous respect for creativity.

It does not matter whether you paint, sculpt, or make shoes; whether you are a gardener, a farmer, a fisherman, a carpenter—it does not matter. What matters is, are you putting your very soul into what you are creating? Then your creative products have something of the quality of divine.

REMEMBER, CREATIVITY HAS NOTHING TO DO WITH ANY PARTICULAR WORK. Creativity has something to do with the quality of your consciousness. Whatsoever you do can become creative. Whatsoever you do can become creative if you know what creativity means.

Creativity means enjoying any work as meditation, doing any work with deep love. If you love, and you clean this auditorium, it is creative. If you don't love, then of course it is a chore, it is a duty to be done some-

> It does not matter whether you paint, sculpt, or make shoes; whether you are a gardener, a farmer, a fisherman, a carpenter— it does not matter. What matters is, are you putting your very soul into what you are creating? Then your creative products have something of the quality of divine.

how, it is a burden. Then you would like some other time to be creative. What will you do in that other time? Can you find a better thing to do? Are you thinking that if you paint, you will feel creative?

But painting is just as ordinary as cleaning the floor. You will be throwing colors on a canvas—here you go on washing the floor, cleaning the floor; what is the difference? Talking to somebody, a friend, and you feel time is being wasted. You would like to write a great book, then you will be creative. But a friend has come! a little gossiping is perfectly beautiful—be creative!

All the great scriptures are nothing but gossips of people who were creative. What do I go on doing here? Gossiping. They will become gospels some day, but originally they are gossips. But I enjoy doing them, I can go on and on for eternity—you may get tired someday, I am not going to get tired, it is sheer delight. It is possible that one day you may get so tired that you disappear and there is nobody—and I will still be talking. If you really love something, it is creative.

But this happens to everybody. Many people come to me, and when they come for the first time they will say, "Any work, Osho. Any work—even cleaning!" Exactly they say, "Even cleaning!— but it is your work and we will be happy." And then after a few days they come to me and they say, "Cleaning . . . We would like to have some great creative work."

Let me tell you one anecdote:

Worried about their lackluster sex life, the young wife finally persuaded her husband to undergo hypnotic treatment. After a few sessions his sexual interest was kindled again, but during their lovemaking he would occasionally dash out of the bedroom, go to the bathroom, and come back again.

Overcome by curiosity, the wife followed him one day to the bathroom. Tiptoeing to the doorway she saw him standing before the mirror staring fixedly at himself and muttering, "She is not my wife. . . . She is not my wife."

When you fall in love with a woman, of course she is not your wife. You make love, you enjoy, but then things settle; then she is your wife. Then things become old. Then you know the face, you know the body, you know the topography, and then you get bored. The hypnotist did well! He simply suggested, While making love to your wife, you go on thinking, "She is not my wife. She is not my wife."

So while cleaning, just go on thinking you are painting. "This is not cleaning, this is great creativity"—and it will be! It is just your mind playing tricks. If you understand, then you bring your creativity to every act that you do.

A man of understanding is continuously creative. Not that he is trying to be creative—the way he sits is a creative act. Watch him sitting; you will find in his movement a certain quality of dance, a certain dignity. Just the other day we were reading the story of the Zen master who stood in the hole, in a grave, with great dignity— dead. Even his death was a creative act. He did it perfectly well, you cannot improve upon it—even dead he was standing with dignity, with grace.

When you understand, whatsoever you do—cooking, cleaning . . . Life consists of small things. Just your ego goes on saying these are small things and you would like some great thing to

> ꙮ
>
> Life consists of small things, just your ego goes on saying these are small things. You would like some great thing to do—a great poetry. You would like to become Shakespeare or Kalidas or Milton. It is your ego that is creating the trouble. Drop the ego and everything is creative.

do—great poetry. You would like to become Shakespeare or Kalidas or Milton. It is your ego that is creating the trouble. Drop the ego and everything is creative.

I have heard:

A housewife was so pleased with the promptness shown by the grocer's boy that she asked him his name. "Shakespeare," replied the boy.

"Well, that is quite a famous name."

"It should be. I have been delivering in this neighborhood for almost three years now."

I like it! Why bother about being Shakespeare? Three years delivering in a neighborhood—it's almost as beautiful as writing a book, a novel, a play.

Life consists of small things. They become great if you love. Then everything is tremendously great. If you don't love, then your ego goes on saying, "This is not worthy of you. Cleaning? This is not worthy of you. Do something great, become Joan of Arc." All nonsense. All Joan of Arcs are nonsense.

Cleaning is great! Don't go on an ego trip. Whenever the ego comes and persuades you toward some great things, immediately become aware and drop the ego, and then by and by you will find the trivial is sacred. Nothing is profane, everything is sacred and holy.

And unless everything becomes holy to you, your life cannot be religious. A holy man is not what you call a saint—a saint may be just on an ego trip, but he will look a saint to you because you think he has done great deeds. A holy man is an ordinary man who loves ordinary life. Chopping wood, carrying water from the well, cooking—whatsoever he touches becomes holy. Not that he is doing great things, but whatsoever he does, he does it greatly.

The greatness is not in the thing done. The greatness is in the consciousness that you bring while you do it. Try. Touch a pebble with great love; it becomes a Kohinoor, a great diamond. Smile, and suddenly you are a king or a queen. Laugh, delight . . .

Each moment of your life has to be transformed by your meditative love.

When I say be creative, I don't mean that you should all go and become great painters and great poets. I simply mean let your life be a painting, let your life be a poem. Always remember it, otherwise the ego is going to land you in some trouble.

Go to the criminals and ask why

> A holy man is an ordinary man who loves ordinary life. Chopping wood, carrying water from the well, cooking—whatsoever he touches becomes holy. Not that he is doing great things, but whatsoever he does, he does it greatly.

they have become criminals—it is because they could not find any great thing to do. They could not become a president of a country—of course, all persons cannot become presidents of a country—so they killed a president; that is easier. They became as famous as the president; They were in all the newspapers with their pictures on the front page.

A man just a few months ago, killed seven persons, and he was asked why—because those seven persons were totally unrelated to him. He wanted to become great, he said, and no newspaper was ready to publish his poems, his articles; they were refused everywhere. Nobody was ready to publish his picture, and life was fleeting, so he killed seven persons. They were not related to him, he was not angry with them; he just wanted to become famous.

> When I say be creative, I don't mean that you should all go and become great painters and great poets. I simply mean let your life be a painting, let your life be a poem.

Your politicians and your criminals are not different types of people. All criminals are political and all politicians are criminal, not only Richard Nixon. Poor Richard Nixon was caught red-handed, that's all. Others seem to be more clever and more cunning.

Mrs. Moskowitz was bursting with pride. "Did you hear about my son Louie?" she asked her neighbor.

"No, what is with your son Louie?"

"He is going to a psychiatrist. Twice each week he is going to a psychiatrist."

"Is that good?"

"Of course it is good. Forty dollars an hour he pays—forty dollars!—and all he talks about is me."

Never allow yourself this tendency for being great, famous, someone bigger than life-size—never. Life-size is perfect. To be exactly life-size, to be just ordinary, is perfectly as it should be. But live that ordinariness in an extraordinary way. That is what a nirvanic consciousness is all about.

Now let me tell you the last thing. If nirvana becomes a great goal for you to achieve, then you will be in a nightmare. Then nirvana can become the last and the greatest nightmare. But if nirvana is in small things, the way you live them—the way you transform every small activity into a holy act, into a prayer . . . your house becomes a temple, your body becomes the abode of God, and wherever you look and whatsoever you touch is tremendously beautiful, sacred—then nirvana is freedom.

Nirvana is to live the ordinary life so alert, so full of consciousness, so full of light, that everything becomes luminous. It is possible. I say so because I have lived it so, I am living it so. When I say it, I say it with authority. When I say it, I am not quoting Buddha or Jesus; when I say it I am quoting only myself.

It has become possible for me; it can become possible for you. Just don't hanker for the ego. Just love life, trust life, and life will give you all that you need. Life will become a blessing for you, a benediction.

4. BE A DREAMER

Friedrich Nietzsche in one of his statements says, "The greatest calamity will fall on humanity the day all the dreamers disappear." The whole evolution of man is because man has dreamed about it. What was a dream yesterday, today is a reality, and what is a dream today can become a reality tomorrow.

All the poets are dreamers, all the musicians are dreamers, all the mystics are dreamers. In fact, creativity is a by-product of dreaming.

But these dreams are not the dreams that Sigmund Freud analyzes. So you have to make a distinction between the dream of a poet, the dream of a sculptor, the dream of an architect, the dream of a mystic, the dream of a dancer—and the dreams of a sick mind.

It is very unfortunate that Sigmund Freud never bothered about the great dreamers who are the foundation of the whole of human evolution. He came across only psychologically sick people, and because his whole life's experience was to analyze the dreams of psychopaths, the very word *dreaming* became condemned. The madman dreams, but his dream is going to be destructive of himself. The creative man also dreams, but his dream is going to enrich the world.

I am reminded of Michelangelo. He was passing through the market where all kinds of marble was available and he saw a beautiful rock, so he inquired about it. The owner said, "If you want that rock, you can take it for free because it has just been lying around taking up space. And for twelve years, nobody has even asked about it; I also don't see that there is any potential in that rock."

Michelangelo took the rock, worked on it for almost the whole year, and made perhaps the most beautiful statue that has ever existed. Just a few years ago a madman tried to destroy it. It was in the Vatican; it was a statue of Jesus Christ after he was taken down from the cross and is lying dead in his mother Mary's lap. I have seen only the photographs of it, but it is so alive, as if Jesus is going to wake up any moment. And he has used the marble with such artfulness that you can feel both things—the strength of Jesus and the fragileness. And the tears are in the eyes of Jesus' mother, Mary.

A madman, just few years ago, hammered the rock that Michelangelo had made, and when he was asked why he had done it he said, "I also want to become famous. Michelangelo had to work one year; then he became famous. I had only to work for five minutes and I destroyed the whole statue. And my name has gone around the world as a headline on all the papers."

Both men worked on the same marble rock. One was a creator, another was a madman.

After one year, when Michelangelo had finished the work, he asked the shopkeeper to come to his home because he wanted to show him something. The shopkeeper could not believe his eyes. He said, "From where did you get this beautiful marble?"

And Michelangelo said, "Don't you recognize? It is the same ugly rock that waited in front of your shop for twelve years." And I remember this incident because the shopkeeper asked, "How did you manage to think that that ugly rock could be turned into such a beautiful statue?"

Michelangelo said, "I did not think about it. I have been dreaming of making this statue, and when I was passing by the rock I suddenly saw Jesus, calling me, 'I am encaged in the rock. Free me; help me to get out of this rock.' I saw exactly the same statue in the rock. So I have only done a small job: I have removed the unnecessary parts of the rock, and Jesus and Mary are free from their bondage."

It would have been a great contribution if a man of the same caliber as Sigmund Freud, instead of analyzing the sick people and their dreams, had worked on the dreams of psychologically healthy, and not only healthy but creative people. The analysis of their dreams will not show that all dreams are repressions. The analysis of their dreams will show that there are dreams that are born out of a more creative consciousness than ordinary people have. And their dreams are not sick, their dreams are authentically healthy. The whole evolution of man and his consciousness depends on these dreamers.

The whole existence is one organic unity. You are not holding hands only with each other, you are holding hands with the trees. You are not only breathing together, the whole universe is breathing together.

The universe is in a deep harmony. Only man has forgotten the language of harmony, and my work here is to remind you. We are not creating harmony; harmony is your reality. It is just that you have forgotten about it. Perhaps it is so obvious that one tends to forget about it. Perhaps you are born in it; how can you think about it?

An ancient parable is that a fish who was of a philosophical bent of mind was asking other fish, "I have heard so much about the ocean; where is it?" And she is in the ocean! But she was born in the ocean, she has lived in the ocean; there has never been any separation. She has not seen ocean as a separate object from herself. An old fish caught hold of the young philosopher and told her, "This is the ocean we are in."

But the young philosopher said, "You must be kidding. This

is water and you are calling it the ocean. I will have to inquire more, of wiser people around."

A fish comes to know about the ocean only when it is caught by a fisherman and drawn out of the ocean, thrown into the sand. Then, for the first time she understands that she has always lived in the ocean, that ocean is her life and without it she cannot survive.

But with man there is a difficulty. You cannot be taken out of existence. Existence is infinite, there are no shores where you can stand aloof and see existence. Wherever you are, you will be part of existence.

We are all breathing together. We are part of one orchestra. To understand it is a great experience—don't call it dreaming, because dreaming has got a very wrong connotation because of Sigmund Freud. Otherwise it is one of the most beautiful words, very poetic.

And just to be silent, just to be joyful, just to be—in this silence, you will feel you are joined with others. When you are thinking, you are separate from others because you are thinking some thoughts and the other person is thinking different thoughts. But if you are both silent, then all the walls between you disappear.

Two silences cannot remain two. They become one.

All great values of life—love, silence, blissfulness, ecstasy, godliness—make you aware of an immense oneness. There is nobody else other than you; we are all different expressions of one reality, different songs of one singer, different dances of one dancer, different paintings—but the painter is one.

But don't call it a dream, because in calling it a dream you are not understanding that it is a reality. And reality is far more beautiful than any dream can be. Reality is more psychedelic, more colorful, more joyful, more dancing than you can ever imagine. But we are living so unconsciously. . . .

> *❧*
>
> When you are thinking, you are separate from others because you are thinking some thoughts and the other person is thinking different thoughts. But if you are both silent, then all the walls between you disappear. Two silences cannot remain two. They become one.

Our first unconsciousness is that we think that we are separate. But I emphasize that no man is an island; we are all part of a vast continent. There is variety, but that does not make us separate. Variety makes life richer—part of us is in the Himalayas, a part of us is in the stars, a part of us is in the roses. A part of us is in the bird on the wing, a part of us is in the green of the trees. We are spread all over. To experience it as reality will transform your whole approach toward life, will transform your every act, will transform your very being.

You will become full of love; you will become full of reverence for life. You will become for the first time, according to me, truly religious—not a Christian, not a Hindu, not a Mohammedan, but truly, purely religious.

The word *religion* is beautiful. It comes from a root that means bringing together those who have fallen apart in their ignorance; bringing them together, waking them up so that they can see they are not separate. Then you cannot hurt even a tree. Then your compassion and your love will be just spontaneous—not cultivated, not something of a discipline. If love is a discipline, it is false. If nonviolence is cultivated, it is false. If compassion is nurtured, it is false. But if they come spontaneously, without any effort of your own, then they have a reality so deep, so exquisite . . .

In the name of religion, so much crime has been done in the past. More people have been killed by religious people than by anybody else. Certainly all these religions have been fake, pseudo.

The authentic religion has to be born.

Once H. G. Wells was asked, when he had published his history of the world—a tremendous work—"What do you think about civilization?"

And he said, "It is a good idea, but somebody should do something to bring it into existence."

> The word *religion* is beautiful. It comes from a root which means bringing together those who have fallen apart in their ignorance, bringing them together, waking them up so that they can see they are not separate.

Up to now we have not been civilized, not cultured, not religious. In the name of civilization, in the name of culture, in the name of religion we have been doing all kinds of barbarous acts—primitive, subhuman, animalistic.

Man has fallen far away from reality. He has to be awakened to the truth that we are all one. And it is not a hypothesis; it is the experience of all the meditators, without exception, down the ages, that the whole existence is one, organic unity.

So don't mistake any beautiful experience as a dream. To call it a dream cancels its reality. Dreams have to be made real, not reality changed into dreams.

FOUR QUESTIONS

❧

You have a song in your heart to be sung and you have a dance to be danced, but the dance is invisible, and the song—even you have not heard it yet. It is deep down hidden in the innermost core of your being; it has to be brought to the surface, it has to be expressed. That's what is meant by "self-actualization."

1. MEMORY AND IMAGINATION

You implore us constantly to give up memory, to live in the herenow. But in giving up memory I must also give up my creative imagination, for I am a writer and all that I write about has its roots in what I remember.

I wonder—what would the world be like without art and the creative imagination that makes art possible? A Tolstoy could never become a Buddha, but then could a Buddha write War and Peace?

You have not understood me, but that's natural. It is impossible to understand me, because to understand me you will have to drop your memory. Your memory interferes. You only listen to my words, and then you go on interpreting those words according to your memory, according to your past. You cannot understand me if you are not herenow . . . only then the meeting. Only in that moment you are with me; otherwise, you are physically present here, psychologically absent.

I have not been telling you to drop your factual memory. That will be stupid! Your factual memory is a must. You must know your name, who your father is and who your mother is and who your wife is and who your child is, and your address; you will have to go back to the hotel, you will have to find your room again. Factual memory is not meant—psychological memory is meant. Factual memory is not a problem, it is pure remembrance. When you become psychologically affected by it, then the problem arises. Try to understand the difference.

Yesterday somebody insulted you. Again he comes across you today. The factual memory is that "this man insulted me yesterday." The psychological memory is that seeing that man you become angry; seeing that man, you start boiling up. And the man may be coming just to apologize; the man may be coming to be excused, to be forgiven. He may have realized his mistake; he may have realized his unconscious behavior. He may be coming to befriend you again, but you become boiled up. You are angry, you start shouting. You don't see his face herenow; you go on being affected by the face that was yesterday. But yesterday is yesterday! How much water has flowed down the Ganges? This man is not the same man. Twenty-four hours have brought many changes—and you are not the same man either.

The factual memory says, "This man insulted me yesterday," but that "me" has changed. This man has changed. So it is as if that incident had happened between two persons with whom you have nothing to do anymore—then you are psychologically free. You don't say, "I still feel angry." There is no lingering anger. Memory is there, but there is no psychological affectation. You meet the man again as he is now, and you meet him as you are now.

A man came and spat on Buddha's face. He was very angry. He was a Brahmin and Buddha was saying things that the priests were very angry about. Buddha wiped off his face and asked the man, "Have you anything more to say?"

His disciple, Ananda, became very angry. He was so angry that he asked Buddha, "Just give me permission to put this man right. This is too much! I cannot tolerate it."

Buddha said, "But he has not spat on your face. This is my face. Second, just look at the man! In what great trouble he is— just look at the man! Feel compassion for him. He wants to say something to me, but words are inadequate. That is my problem also, my whole life's long problem—and I see the man in the same situation! I want to relate things to you that I have come to know, but I cannot relate them because words are inadequate. This man is in the same boat: he is so angry that no word can express his anger—just as I am in so much love that no word, no act, can express it. I see this man's difficulty—just see!"

Buddha is seeing, Ananda is also seeing. Buddha is simply collecting a factual memory; Ananda is creating a psychological memory.

The man could not believe his ears, what Buddha was saying. He was very much shocked. He would not have been shocked if Buddha had hit him back, or Ananda had jumped upon him. There would have been no shock; that would have been expected, that would have been natural. That's how human beings react. But Buddha feeling for the man, seeing his difficulty . . . The man went, could not sleep the whole night, pondered over it, meditated over it. Started feeling a great hurt, started feeling what he had done. A wound opened in his heart.

Early in the morning, he rushed to Buddha's feet, fell at Buddha's feet, kissed his feet. And Buddha said to Ananda, "Look, again the same problem! Now he is feeling so much for me, he cannot speak in words. He is touching my feet. Man is so helpless. Anything that is too much cannot be expressed, cannot be conveyed, cannot be communicated. Some gesture has to be found to symbolize it. Look!"

And the man started crying and said, "Excuse me, sir. I am immensely sorry. It was absolute stupidity on my part to spit on you, a man like you."

Buddha said, "Forget about it! The man you spat upon is no more, and the man who spat is no more. You are new, I am new! Look—this sun that is rising is new. Everything is new. The yesterday is no more. Be finished with it! And how can I forgive? because you never spat on me. You spat on somebody who has departed."

Consciousness is a continuous river.

When I say drop your memory, I mean psychological memory; I don't mean factual memory. Buddha remembers perfectly that yesterday this man had spat on him, but he also remembers that neither is this man the same nor is he the same. That chapter is closed; it is not worth carrying it your whole life. But you go on carrying. Somebody had said something to you ten years before and you are still carrying it. Your mother was angry when you were a child and you are still carrying it. Your father had slapped you when you were just small and you are still carrying it, and you may be seventy years old.

These psychological memories go on burdening you. They destroy your freedom, they destroy your aliveness, they encage you. Factual memory is perfectly okay.

And one thing more to be understood: when there is no psychological memory, the factual memory is very accurate—because the psychological memory is a disturbance. When you are very much psychologically disturbed, how can you remember accurately? It is impossible! You are trembling, you are shaking, you are in a kind of earthquake—how can you remember exactly? You will exaggerate; you will add something, you will delete something, you will make something new out of it. You cannot be relied upon.

A man who has no psychological memory can be relied upon. That's why computers are more reliable than men, because they have no psychological memory. Just the facts— bare facts, naked facts. When you talk about a fact, then too it is not fact: much fiction has entered into it. You have molded it, you have changed it, you have painted it, you have given it colors of your own it is no more a fact! Only a Buddha, a *tathagata*, an enlightened person, knows what a fact is; you never come across a fact, because you carry so many fictions in your mind. Whenever

> When there is no psychological memory, the factual memory is very accurate—because the psychological memory is a disturbance. When you are very much psychologically disturbed, how can you remember accurately? It is impossible.

you find a fact, you immediately impose your fictions on it. You never see that which is, you go on distorting reality.

Buddha says a *tathagata*, an awakened one, is always true because he speaks in accordance with reality. A *tathagata* speaks truth, never otherwise. A *tathagata* is synonymous with suchness. Whatsoever it is, a *tathagata* simply reflects; it is a mirror. That's what I mean—drop psychological memories and you will become a mirror.

You have asked, "You implore us constantly to give up memory, to live in the here and now. . . ." That does not mean that your past cannot be remembered. Past is part of the present; whatsoever you have been in the past, whatsoever you have done in the past, is part of your present, it is *here*. Your child is in you, your young man is in you . . . all that you have been doing is in you. The food that you have eaten—it is past, but it has become your blood; it is circulating herenow, it has become your bone, it has become your marrow. The love that you went through may be past but it has transformed you. It has given you a new vision of life, it has opened your eyes. Yesterday you were with me—it is past, but is it really totally past? How can it be totally past? You were changed by it; you were given a new spark, a new fire—that has become part of you.

Your present moment contains your whole past. And if you can understand me, your present moment also contains your whole future—because the past as it has happened has been changing you, it has been preparing you. And the future that is going to happen will happen from the way you live in the present. The way you live herenow will have a great impact upon your future.

In the present moment all past is contained, and in the present moment all future is potential—but you need not be psychologically worried about it. It is already there! You need not carry it psychologically, you need not be burdened by it. If you understand me, that it is contained in the present already . . . the tree is not thinking about the water that it soaked up yesterday, but it is there! Thinking or not thinking. And the sun rays that fell on it yesterday—it is not thinking about them. Trees are not so foolish, not as stupid as men.

Why bother about the rays of yesterday? They have been absorbed, digested; they have become part the green, the red, and the gold. The tree is enjoying *this* morning's sun, with no psychological memory of yesterday. Although the yesterday is contained in the leaves, in the flowers, in the branches, in the roots, in the sap. It is there! And the future is also coming; the new buds, which will become flowers tomorrow, are there. And the small new leaves that will become foliage tomorrow are there, on the way.

The present moment contains all. Now is eternity.

So I am not saying to forget the factual past; I am simply saying don't be disturbed by it anymore. It should not be a psychological investment. It is a physical fact—let it be so. And I am not saying become incapable of remembering it—it may be needed! When it is needed, the need is in the present, remember, and you have to respond to the need. Somebody asks you your phone number—the need is present because somebody is asking now, and you say, "How can I tell you my phone number? Because I have dropped my past." Then you will get into unnecessary troubles. Your life, rather than becoming free, rather than becoming a great joy and celebration, will be hampered at every step; you will find a thousand and one problems unnecessarily being created by you. There is no need.

Try to understand me.

And you say, "But in giving up memory I must also give up my creative imagination . . ." What does memory have to do with creative imagination? In fact, the more memory you have, the less creative you will be—because you will go on repeating the memory, and creativity means allowing the new to happen. Allowing the new to happen means putting aside the memory so the past does not interfere.

Let the new penetrate you. Let the new come and thrill your heart. The past will be needed, but not now; the past will be needed when you start expressing this new experience. Then the past will be needed because the language will be needed—language comes from the past. You cannot invent language right now—or if you do invent it, it will be gibberish; it will not mean anything. And it will not be a communication, it will be talking in tongues, it will be baby talk. Not much creativity will come out of it. You will be talking nonsense.

To talk sense, language is needed; language comes from the past. But language should come only when the experience has happened! Then use it as a tool. It should not hinder you.

When you see the rose opening in the early morning sun, *see* it. Let it have an impact, allow it to go deep in you. Let its rosiness overpower you, overwhelm you. Don't say anything, wait. Be patient, be open. Absorb. Let the rose reach you, and you reach the rose. Let there be a meeting, a communion of two beings—the rose and you. Let there be a penetration, an interpenetration.

And remember: the deeper the rose goes in you, the deeper you can go into the rose; it is always in the same proportion. A moment comes when you don't know who is the rose and who is the spectator. A moment comes when you become the rose and the rose becomes you, when the observer is the observed, when all duality disappears. In that moment you will know the reality, the suchness of the rose. Then catch hold of your language, catch hold of your art. If you are a painter, then take your brush and color and your canvas, and paint it. If you are a poet, then rush into your factual memory for the right words so that you can express this experience.

But while the experience is happening, don't go on talking inside yourself. The inner talk will be an interference. You will never know the rose in its intensity and depth. You will know only the superficial, the shallow. And if you know the shallow, the shallow is going to be your expression; your art will not be of much value.

You say, "But in giving up memory I must also give up my creative imagination . . ." You don't understand the meaning of creative. Creative means the new, the novel, the original. Creative means the fresh, the unknown. You have to be open for it, vulnerable for it.

Put aside the memory. Its use is later on. Right now it will be an interference.

Right now, for instance, you are listening to me—put your memory aside. When you are listening to me, are you repeating inside yourself all the mathematics that you know? Are you counting figures inside? Are you repeating the geography that you know? Are you repeating history that you know? You have put them aside. Do the same with language too, as

> Creative means the new, the novel, the original. Creative means the fresh, the unknown. You have to be open for it, vulnerable for it. Put aside the memory.

you do with history and mathematics and geography. Do the same with language—do the same with your memory, put it aside! It will be needed—but when it is needed, only then use it. Put the whole mind aside!

You are not destroying the mind, you are simply giving it a rest. It is not needed, you can give it a holiday. You can say to the mind, "Rest for one hour and let me listen. And when I have listened, when I have absorbed, when I have eaten and drunk, then I will recall you, then your help will be needed—your language, your knowledge, your information will be needed. Then I am going to paint a picture or write a poem or write a book, but right now you can rest." And the mind will be fresher after a rest. You don't allow the mind rest; that's why your mind remains mediocre.

Just think of a man who wants to participate in an Olympic race and he continuously goes on running, twenty-four hours a day, preparing for the Olympic race. By the time the race happens he will not even be able to move, he will be so dead tired. Before the race you will have to rest, you will have to get as deep a rest as possible so the body is rejuvenated.

Exactly the same has to be done with the mind. Creative imagination has nothing to do with memory—only then is it creative. If you understand me, and you drop psychological memory, you will become creative. Otherwise, what you call creation is not really creation—it is just a composition. There is a great difference between creation and composition. You go on arranging your old known things in different ways, but they are old; nothing is new there. You simply manage to change the structure.

It is like arranging your drawing room—the furniture is the same, the pictures on the wall are the same, the curtains are the same, but you can arrange them again. You can put this chair there and that table here, and you can change this picture from this wall to the other. It may look new, but it is not new. It is a composition; you have not created anything. That's what ninety-nine percent of authors, poets, painters go on doing. They are mediocre; they are not creative.

The creative person is one who brings something from the unknown into the world of the known, who brings something from God into the world, who helps God to utter something—who becomes a hollow bamboo and allows God to flow through him. How can you become a hollow bamboo? If you are too full of the mind, you cannot become a hollow bamboo. And creativity is from the creator, creativity is not of you or from you. You disappear, then creativity is—when the creator takes possession of you.

The real creators know it perfectly well, that they are not the creators—they were just instrumental, they were mediums. Something happened through them, true, but they are not the doers of it.

Remember the difference between a technician and a creative person. A technician just knows how to do a thing. Maybe he knows perfectly how to do a thing, but he has no insight. A creative person is one who has insight, who can see things that nobody has ever seen before, who can see things that no eye has ever been able to see, who hears things that nobody has heard before. Then there is creativity.

Just see. . . . Jesus' statements are creative—nobody has spoken like that before. He is not an educated person. He knows nothing of the skill of speaking, he knows nothing about eloquence—but he is eloquent as rarely, very few people, ever have been. What is his secret? He has insight. He has looked into God, he has looked into the unknown. He has encountered the unknown and the unknowable. He has been into that space, and from that space he brings a few fragments. Only fragments can be brought, but when you bring some fragments from the unknowable you transform the whole quality of human consciousness on the earth.

He is creative. I will call him an artist. Or a Buddha, or a Krishna, or a Lao Tzu—these are real artists! They make the impossible happen. The impossible is the meeting of the known with the unknown, the meeting of the mind with the no-mind—that is the impossible. They make it happen.

> The real creators know it perfectly well, that they are not the creators—they were just instrumental, they were mediums. Something happened through them, true, but they are not the doers of it.

You say, "But in giving up memory I must also give up my creative imagination. . . ." No. That has nothing to do with creative imagination. In fact, if you put your memory aside you will have creative imagination. You cannot have creative imagination if you are too much burdened by the memory.

You say, ". . . for I am a writer and all that I write about has its roots in what I remember." Then you are not much of a writer. Then you go on writing about the past, then you go on writing memoirs. You don't bring the future in, you go on writing records. You are a file keeper! You can become a writer, but then you will have to make contact with the unknown—not that which you remember. The remembered is already dead. You will have to make contact with that which *is*, not that which you remember. You will have to make contact with the suchness that surrounds you. You will have to go deep into the present so that something of the past also can be caught in your net.

The real creativity is not out of remembrance but out of consciousness. You will have to become more conscious. The more conscious you are, the bigger the net you have, and of course the more fish will be caught.

You say, "I wonder—what would the world be like without art and the creative imagination that makes art possible?" Ninety-nine percent of art is just not art at all; it is rubbish. Rarely is there a work of art, very rarely. Others are just imitators, technicians—skillful people, clever people, but not artists. And that ninety-nine percent of art disappearing from the earth will be a blessing, because it is more like a vomit rather than anything creative.

Now there is something very meaningful around—art therapy. It is meaningful, it has got the point. When people are ill, mentally ill, art can be of help. A mentally ill person can be given canvases and colors and brush and told to paint whatsoever he wants to paint. Of course whatsoever he paints will be mad, maddening. But after painting a few mad things, you will be surprised that he is coming back to sanity. That painting has been like a catharsis; it was a vomit. His system has thrown it out.

Now, the so-called modern art is nothing but that. Picasso's paintings may have saved Picasso from becoming mad, but that's all there is to it. And they are dangerous for you to meditate upon because if you meditate upon somebody's vomit, you will go mad. Avoid! Never keep a Picasso painting in your bedroom, otherwise you will have nightmares.

Just think: keep the Picasso painting for fifteen minutes in front of you and go on looking at it . . . and you will start feeling rest-lessness, discomfort, giddy, nauseous. What is happening? It is somebody's vomit! It has helped him, it was good for him, but it is not good for others.

Look at a Michelangelo and you can meditate for hours. And the more you meditate, the more silent and peaceful you will be-come. It is not a vomit. He has brought something from the un-known. It is not his madness that he has thrown out of his system through the painting or through the sculpture or through the poetry or through music. It is not that he was ill and that he wanted to get rid of his illness, no. It was just the opposite: he was pregnant, not ill. He was pregnant—pregnant with God. Something had taken root in his being and he wanted to share it. It is a fruitfulness, a fulfillment. He has lived in a creative way, he has loved life in a creative way. He has allowed life to enter into his deepest shrine, and there he has become pregnant with life, or pregnant with God. And when you are pregnant, you have to give birth.

Picasso is vomiting, Michelangelo is giving birth. Nietzsche is vomiting, Buddha is giving birth. There is as much difference be-tween these two as there can be. To give birth to a child is one thing, and to vomit is another.

Beethoven is giving birth, something immensely valuable is descending through him. Listening to his music you will be trans-formed, you will be transported into another world. He will give you a few glimpses of the other shore.

Ninety-nine percent of modern art is pathological. If it disap-pears from the world it will be very healthy, it will be helpful. It will not harm. The modern mind is an angry mind—angry because you cannot contact your being, angry because you have lost all meaning, angry because you don't know what significance is.

One of the famous books of Jean Paul Sartre is *Nausea*. That is the state of the modern mind; the modern mind is nauseated, in a great torture. And the torture is its own creation.

Friedrich Nietzsche declared God is dead. The day he declared God is dead, he started becoming insane—because by your declaration that God is dead . . . God cannot be dead just by your declaration. Your declaration does not make any difference. But the moment Nietzsche started believing this, that God is dead, he started dying, he started losing his sanity. A world without a God is bound to be an insane world—because a world without God will not have any context in which to become significant.

Just watch. . . . You read a poem; those words in the poem have meaning only in the context of the poem. If you take a word out of the context, it has no meaning. It was so beautiful in the context! You cut out a piece of a painting, and it has no meaning, because it has lost its roots in the context. In the painting it was so beautiful; it was fulfilling some purpose, it had some meaning. Now it has no meaning.

You can take one of my eyes out of its socket, and it will be a dead eye, and there will be no meaning in it. Right now if you look into my eyes, there is great meaning—because they exist in my total context; they are part of a poetry, they are part of a bigger painting. Meaning is always in reference to something bigger than you.

The day Nietzsche declared there is no God and God is dead, he fell out of context. Without God man cannot have any significance, because man is a small word in the great epic of God, man is a small note in the great orchestra of God. That small single note will be monotonous; it will be jarring to the ears, it will be maddening.

That's what happened to Nietzsche. He authentically believed in his own statement. He was a believer, a believer who believes in himself. He believed that God is dead and man is free—but he simply became mad, not free. And this century has followed Friedrich Nietzsche in a thousand and one ways, and the whole century has gone mad. There has never been any other century in world history that was so mad as this century. Future historians will write of it as the age of madness. It is mad—mad because it has lost context.

Why are you alive? For what? You shrug your shoulders. That does not help much. You look accidental. If you were not, there would have been no difference. If you are, there is no difference. You don't make any difference! You are unneeded. You are not fulfilling anything here. Your being or your not being is all the same. How can you feel happy, and how can you remain sane? Accidental? Just accidental? Then anything is right, then murder is right! Because if everything is accidental then what does it matter what you do? No action carries any value—then suicide is okay, then murder is okay, then everything is okay!

But everything is not okay—because there are a few things that give you joy and a few things that make you miserable, a few things that create ecstasy and a few things that create only agony, a few things that create only hell and a few things that take you to a world of paradise. No, all things are not the same. But once God is thought to be dead, once you lose contact with the totality—and God is nothing but the totality. . . . What is a wave when it has forgotten about the ocean? Then it is nothing. It was a great tidal wave when it was part of the ocean.

Remember: the real art arises out of real religiousness, because religiousness is finding a communion with reality. Once you are in communion with reality, then real art arises.

You say, "I wonder—what would the world be like without art and the creative imagination that makes art possible?"

If the ninety percent so-called art disappears, the world will be far richer—because then there will be real art. If these mad pretenders go . . . and I am not saying that they should not paint—they should paint, but as therapy. It is therapeutic. Picasso needs therapy; he should paint, but those paintings should not be on exhibition—or if they are, then only in madhouses. They may help a few mad people to have a release; they are cathartic.

Real art means something that helps you to be meditative. Gurdjieff used to call real art objective art—that helps you to meditate. The Taj Mahal is real art. Have you gone to the Taj Mahal? It is worth going to. On a full-moon night, just sitting there and looking at that beautiful masterpiece you will be filled with the unknown. You will start feeling something from the beyond.

I would like to tell you the story of how the Taj Mahal came into existence.

A man came from Shiraz, Iran. He was called Shirazi because he had come from Shiraz. He was a great artist, the most famous from Shiraz. And he was a miracle man; a thousand and one stories had come before he came to India. Shah Jehan was the emperor; he heard about those stories. He invited the sculptor to come to the court. And Shirazi was a mystic, a Sufi mystic.

Shah Jehan asked him, "I have heard that you can sculpt the whole body of a man or a woman just by touching his or her hand and not seeing his or her face at all. Is it true?"

Shirazi said, "Give me a chance—but with one condition. Put twenty-five beautiful women from your palace behind a screen, behind a curtain. Let their hands simply be available to me outside the curtain. I will touch their hands and I will choose the person—

but with one condition. Whomsoever I choose I will make an image of: if the image comes absolutely true and you are satisfied, your whole court is satisfied, then that woman will be my woman; I want to get married to her; I want a woman from your palace."

Shah Jehan was ready. He said, "That's perfectly okay."

Twenty-five slave girls, beautiful slave girls, were put behind a curtain. He went from the first to the second to the twenty-fifth, rejecting all. Just out of playfulness, Shah Jehan's daughter, just to play a joke, was also standing behind the screen—when twenty-five were rejected, she put out her hand. He touched her hand, closed his eyes, felt something, and said, "This is my hand." And he put a ring on the daughter's hand to signify that "If I succeed, then she is going to be my wife."

The emperor reached behind the screen and he was terrified: "What has this girl done?" But he was not worried because it was almost impossible to make a statue of the whole woman just by touching her hand.

For three months, Shirazi disappeared into a room; day and night he worked. And after three months he asked the emperor and the whole court to come—and the emperor could not believe his eyes. It was exactly the same! He *was* capable. He could not find a single fault—he wanted to find a fault, because he was not willing that his daughter should be married to a poor man, but now there was no way. He had given his word.

He was disturbed, and his wife was so disturbed that she fell ill. She was pregnant, and while giving birth to the child, she died—out of agony. Her name was Mumtaj Mahal.

And the king became so desperate—how to save his daughter? He asked the sculptor to come, and he told him the whole thing, "It has been a mistake. And the girl is at fault, but look at my situation: my wife has died and the reason is that she could not agree to the idea of her daughter going with a poor man. And I cannot agree either—although I have given you my promise."

The sculptor, the artist, said, "There is no need to be so worried. You should have told me, I will go back. No need to be worried. I will not ask; I will go back to Shiraz. Forget about it!"

But the king said, "That is not possible; I cannot forget. I have given you a promise, my word. You wait. Let me think."

The prime minister suggested, "You do one thing: your wife has died and this is a great artist and he has proved himself—tell him to make a model in the memory of your wife. You should create a beautiful tomb, the most beautiful in the world. And make it a condition that if you approve of his model, then you will have to give your daughter to him in marriage. If you don't approve, it is finished."

The matter was talked over with the artist and he was willing; he said, "Perfectly okay."

"Now," the king thought, "I will never approve."

And Shirazi made many models, and they were so beautiful, but still the king persisted and said, "No, no, no."

The prime minister became desperate, because those models were rare. Each model was rare, and to say no to it was unjust. He rumored around, particularly to the sculptor, "The girl that you have chosen, the daughter of the king, is very ill." For one week she was very ill, then the next week she became very very ill, and the third week she died—in the rumors.

When the rumor reached the sculptor that the girl had died, he made his last model. The girl was dead, his heart was broken. And this was going to be the last model. He brought it to the king and he approved of it. The trick was that the girl was dead so there was no question of marrying.

That model became the Taj Mahal. That model was created by a Sufi mystic. How could he create the whole image of the woman just by touching her hand once? He must have been in a different kind of space. He must have been in that moment without mind. That moment must have been a moment of great meditation. In that moment he touched the energy, and just by feeling the energy he created the whole shape.

Now this can be understood far more logically because of Kirlian photography, because each energy has its own pattern. Your face is not accidental; your face is there because you have a particular energy pattern. Your eyes, your hair, your color—all are there because you have a particular energy pattern.

Meditators have been working on energy patterns down the ages. Once you know the energy pattern, you know the whole personality. You know in and out, all—because it is the energy pattern that creates everything. You know past, you know present, you know future. Once the energy pattern has been understood, there is the key, the nucleus, of all that has happened to you and all that is going to happen.

This is objective art. This man created the Taj Mahal.

On a full-moon night, meditating on the Taj Mahal, your heart will throb with new love. The Taj Mahal carries that energy of love still. Mumtaj Mahal died because of her love for the daughter; Shah Jehan suffered because of the love; and this Shirazi created this model because he suffered deeply, he was wounded deeply, because his future was dark. The woman he had chosen was no more. Out of great love and meditativeness the Taj Mahal came into existence.

It still carries the vibe. It is not an ordinary monument, it is special. So are the pyramids in Egypt, and there are many, many things in the world created as objective art—created by those who knew what they were doing, created by great meditators. So are the Upanishads, so are the sutras of Buddha, so are Jesus' statements.

Remember, to me, creativity means meditativeness, creativity means a state of no-mind—then God descends in you, then love flows out of you. Then something happens out of your well-being, overflowing well-being. It is a blessing. Otherwise it is a vomit.

You can paint, you can write as a therapy, but burn your paintings and burn your poetry. You need not go on exhibiting your vomit to people. And the people who become interested in your vomit must be ill themselves; they also need therapy—because if you become interested in something you show who you are, where you are.

I am all for objective art, I am all for a meditative art, I am all for something from God to descend. You become the vehicle.

And you say, "A Tolstoy could never become a Buddha." Who has told you this? A Tolstoy *can* become a Buddha, *will* become a Buddha sooner or later.

And you say, "But then could a Buddha write *War and Peace*?" And what has Buddha been doing? What am I doing here? Have you read Krishna's Gita?—it is *War and Peace*! Tolstoy could write *War and Peace, Anna Karenina*, and many other

> You can paint, you can write as a therapy, but burn your paintings and burn your poetry. You need not go on exhibiting your vomit to people.

beautiful things, not because he was Tolstoy but in spite of being a Tolstoy. Dostoyevsky has written *The Idiot, Crime and Punishment*, and one of the most beautiful things, *The Brothers Karamazov*—not because he was Dostoyevsky but in spite of it. Something of him was that of a Buddha; something of him was immensely religious. Dostoyevsky was a religious man—not totally, but a part, a fragment of him, was immensely religious. That's why *The Brothers Karamazov* has such a beautiful quality in it. It is not just out of an ordinary man; something has come from the divine. Dostoyevsky has been taken possession of by the God, he has become a vehicle. Of course, he is not a perfect vehicle, so many things go on from his mind. Still, *The Brothers Karamazov* is beautiful. If there had been no Dostoyevsky, no memory, no ego, no pathology, then *The Brothers Karamazov* would have been another New Testament; it would have been the same as Jesus' statements or a Diamond Sutra or a Upanishad. He has the quality!

2. POSTPARTUM DEPRESSION

When I am writing a book, I am full of flowing energy and delight. But when I have finished, I am so empty and dead that I can hardly bear to live. Now I am just starting to write, but though I can get into the pleasure while I am working, during meditation I get overwhelmed with fear of the emptiness that I expect months from now.

This question is from a novelist. I have gone through her novels and they are beautiful. She has the knack of it—how to tell a story beautifully, how to weave a story. And this experience is not only hers, it is the experience of almost everybody who is in any way creative. But still, the interpretation is wrong, and much depends on the interpretation.

When a woman carries a child, she is full. Of course, when the child is born, she will feel empty. She will miss the new life that was throbbing and kicking in her womb. The child has gone out; she will feel empty for a few days. But she can love the child, and she can forget her emptiness in loving the child and helping the child to grow. For an artist, even that is not possible. You paint, or you write a poem or a novel; once it is finished you feel deep emptiness. And what can you do with the book now? So the artist is in an even more difficult situation than a mother. Once a book is finished, it is finished—now it needs no help, no love. It is not going to grow. It is perfect, it is born grown up. A painting is finished, it is finished. An artist feels very empty. But one has to look into this emptiness. Don't say that you are exhausted; rather, say that you are spent. Don't say that you are empty, because each emptiness also has a fullness in it. You are looking from the wrong end.

You come into a room, there is furniture, pictures on the walls, and things. Then those things and the pictures are removed and you come into the room—now what will you say? Will you call it empty or will you call it a full room? *Room* means "emptiness"; *room* means "space." With the furniture removed, the room is full. When furniture was there the room was not full; much of it was missing because of the furniture. Now the room is complete, the emptiness is total.

You can look from two ends. If you are too furniture oriented, so that you can look only at the chairs and tables and the sofa and you cannot see the roominess of the room, then it will feel empty. But if you know, and you can see emptiness directly, you will feel a tremendous freedom, which was not there before because the room was missing; you could not move in it. Go on filling it with furniture and there will come a point when you cannot move because the whole room is gone.

Once I stayed in a very rich man's house. He was very rich, but had no taste. His house was so full that it was not a house at all. You could not move, and you were always afraid to move because he had precious antiques. He himself was afraid to move. The servants were constantly worried. He gave me the best, the most beautiful room in his house. And I told him, "This is not a room, it is a museum. Please give me something where I can move; then it will be a room. This is not a room. The room has almost disappeared!"

The room means the freedom that space gives you. When you are working, creating, your mind is full of many things. The mind is occupied. Writing a novel the mind is occupied, writing a poem the mind is occupied. There is too much furniture in it, the furniture of the mind—thoughts, feelings, characters. Then the book is finished. Suddenly, the furniture is gone. You feel empty. But there is no need to become sad. If you look at it rightly—this is what Buddha called right-vision, *samyak drasthi*—if you look rightly you will feel freed of an obsession, of an occupation. You will feel clean again, unburdened. Those characters of the novel are no longer moving there. Those guests are gone and the host is totally at ease. Enjoy it! Your wrong interpretation is creating sadness for you and fear. Enjoy it—have you never observed that when a guest comes you feel good, and when he goes you feel even better? He leaves you alone, and now you have your own space.

To write a novel is maddening because so many characters become guests, and each character has his own way. It is not always that he listens to the writer, not always. Sometimes he has his own way and he forces the writer in a certain direction. The writer starts the novel, but never ends it. Those characters end it by themselves.

It is just like giving birth to a child. You can give birth to a child, but then the child starts moving on his own. The mother may have been thinking that the child would become a doctor, and he becomes a hobo—what can you do? You try hard, but he becomes a hobo.

The same happens when you write a novel: you start with a character—you were going to make a saint out of him, and he becomes a sinner. And I tell you, it is exactly as it happens to a child: the mother is worried, the novelist is worried. The novelist wanted him to become a saint and he is becoming a sinner, and nothing can be done. He feels almost helpless, almost used by these characters. They are his fantasies—but once you cooperate with them they become almost real. And unless you get rid of them, you will never be at peace. If you have a book in your mind, it has to be written to get rid of it. It is a catharsis, it is unburdening yourself.

That's why creative people almost always go mad. Mediocrities never go mad—they have nothing to go mad over, they have nothing maddening in their lives. Creators almost always go mad. A Van Gogh will go mad, a Nijinsky will go mad, a Nietzsche will go mad. Why does it happen that they go mad? Because they are so occupied, so many things are happening in the mind. They don't have a space of their own within themselves. So many people are staying there, coming and going. It is almost as if they are sitting on a road and the traffic continues. Each artist has to pay for it.

Remember, when a book is finished and a child is born, feel happy—enjoy that space, because sooner or later a new book will arise. As leaves come out of trees, as flowers come out of trees—

exactly like that, poems come out of a poet, novels come out of a novelist, paintings come out of a painter, songs are born out of a singer. Nothing can be done, they are natural.

So sometimes in the fall when the leaves have fallen and the tree stands alone without leaves against the sky, enjoy it. Don't call it emptiness, call it a new type of fullness—full with yourself. There is nobody to interfere, you are resting in yourself. That period of rest is needed for every artist; it is a natural process. Each mother's body needs a little rest. One child is born and another is conceived . . . it used to happen, it used to happen in the East, and in India it still continues. A woman is almost old by the age of thirty, continuously giving birth to children with no gap to recuperate, to rejuvenate her being, to be alone. She is exhausted, tired. Her youth, her freshness, her beauty, are gone. A rest period is needed when you give birth to a child. You need a rest period. And if the child is going to be a lion, then a long rest period is needed. A lion gives birth to only one child, because the whole being is involved in it. And then there is a rest period, a long rest period to recoup, to regain the energy that you have given to the child—to regain yourself again so that something can be born out of you.

When you write a novel, if it has been really a great piece of art, then you will feel empty. If it has been just a sort of journalism that you have made for money because some publisher has made a contract with you, then it is not very deep. You will not feel empty after it, you will remain the same. The deeper your creation, the greater will be your emptiness afterward. The greater the storm, the greater will be the silence that comes in its wake. Enjoy it. The storm is good, enjoy it; and the silence that follows it is also good. The day is beautiful, full of activity; night is also very beautiful, full of inactivity, passivity, emptiness. One sleeps. In the morning you

> 🙥
>
> The deeper your creation, the greater will be your emptiness afterward. The greater the storm, the greater will be the silence that comes in its wake. Enjoy it. The storm is good, enjoy it, and the silence that follows it is also good.

are again back in the world with full energy to work, to act.

Don't be afraid of the night. Many people are. There is one sannyasin, I have given her the name Nisha. *Nisha* means "the night." She comes to me again and again, and she says, "Please change my name." Why? She says, "I am afraid of night. Why have you given me, out of so many names, just this name? Change it." But I am not going to change it. I have given it to her knowingly, because of her fear—her fear of darkness, her fear of passivity, her fear of relaxation, her fear of surrender. That is all indicated in the word *night, nisha.*

One has to accept the night also. Only then do you become complete, full, whole.

So don't take it amiss. That emptiness is beautiful, more beautiful than the days of creativity—because that creativity comes out of emptiness, those flowers come out of emptiness. Enjoy that emptiness, feel blissful and blessed. Accept it, welcome it like a benediction, and soon you will see that you are again full of activity and a greater book is going to be born. Don't be worried about it. There is no need to worry. It is just a misinterpretation of a beautiful phenomenon.

But man lives in words. Once you call a thing by a wrong name, you start becoming afraid of it. Be very, very exact. Always remember what you say, because saying is not just saying; it has deep associations in your being. Once you call a thing emptiness, you become afraid—the very word.

In India, we have better words for emptiness. We call it *shunya*. The very word is positive; it has nothing of negativity in it. It is beautiful, it simply means space, with no boundaries—*shunya*. And we have called the ultimate goal *shunya*. Buddha says when you become *shunya*, when you become absolutely nothing, a nothingness, then you have attained.

A poet, an artist, a painter, is on the way to becoming a mystic. All artistic activity is on the way toward becoming religious. When you are active, writing a poem, you are in the mind. When the poem is born, you are spent, and the mind takes rest. Use these moments to fall into your being. Don't call it emptiness, call it wholeness; call it being, call it truth, call it God. And then you will be able to feel the benediction of it.

3. CREATIVITY AND CROSSBREEDING

I feel an urge for artistic expression and have had a disciplined, classical training in western music. Often I feel this training imprisons spontaneous creativity, and I have found it very difficult to practice regularly lately. I am not sure anymore what the qualities of true art are and by which process the artist produces and delivers authentic art. How can I feel the artist in me?

The paradox of art is that first you have to learn its discipline and then you have to forget it totally. If you don't know its ABC you will not be able to move very deep into it. But if you know

> ᐳᕫ
>
> A poet, an artist, a painter, is on the way to becoming a mystic. All artistic activity is on the way toward becoming religious.

only its technique and you go on practicing the technique your whole life, you may become very skillful technically, but you will remain a technician; you will never become an artist.

In Zen they say if you want to be a painter, for twelve years learn how to paint and then for twelve years forget all about painting. Just completely forget—it has nothing to do with you. For twelve years meditate, chop wood, carry water from the well. Do anything, but not painting.

And then one day you will be able to paint. Twenty-four years training: twelve years training in learning the technique and twelve years training in forgetting the technique. And then you can paint. Now the technique has become just a part of you; it is no longer technical knowledge, it has become part of your blood and bones and marrow. Now you can be spontaneous. It will not hinder you, it will not imprison you.

That's exactly my experience, too.

Now don't go on practicing. Forget all about classical music. Do other kinds of things: gardening, sculpture, painting, but forget about classical music, as if it does not exist at all. For a few years let it remain deep down in your being so that it becomes digested. It is no longer a technique then. Then one day a sudden urge will take possession of you—and then start playing again. And when you play again, don't be bothered too much about the technique, otherwise you will never be spontaneous.

Be a little innovative—that's what creativity is. Innovate new ways, new means. Try something new that nobody has ever done. The greatest creativity happens in people whose training is of some other discipline.

For example, if a mathematician starts playing music he will bring something new to the world of music. If a musician becomes a mathematician he will bring something new to the world of mathematics. All great creativity happens through people who move from one discipline to another. It is like cross-breeding. And children that come out of crossbreeding are far healthier, far more beautiful.

That's why in every country for centuries, marriages between brothers and sisters have been prohibited; there is a reason in it. A marriage is better if it is between people who are very distantly related or not related at all as far as blood is concerned. It will be good if people from one race marry into another race—and if someday we discover people on some other planet, the best way will be a crossbreeding between earth and the other planet! Then newer kinds of people will be coming into existence.

> Be a little innovative—that's what creativity is. Innovate new ways, new means. Try something new that nobody has ever done. The greatest creativity happens in people whose training is of some other discipline.

The prohibition, the taboo against the brother-sister relationship, their marriage, is significant—scientifically significant. But it has not been worked out into detail to its extreme, to its logical extreme. The logical extreme is that no Indian should marry another Indian, no German should marry another German. The best thing is that a German marries an Indian, an Indian marries a Japanese, a Japanese marries an African, an African marries an American, a Jew marries a Christian, a Christian marries a Hindu, a Hindu marries a Mohammedan. That will be the best thing. That will raise the consciousness of the whole planet. It will give better children, more alert, more alive, richer in every possible way.

But we are so foolish that we can do anything, we can accept anything. Then what am I saying?

Chauncey, a handsome young man, was speaking earnestly with his mother.

"Mother, the time has come—it really has—when we must have a heart-to-heart talk about my relationship with Myron. To be quite candid about it, our relationship has blossomed into—how shall I say it without sounding indelicate?—into something beautiful and good and even holy. The truth is, Mother dear, I love Myron and Myron loves me in return. We want to be married as soon as possible, and we both hope you will give us your blessings."

"But, Chauncey," the mother protested, "do you realize what you are saying? Can you honestly expect me to condone such a marriage? What will people say? What will our friends and neighbors think?"

"Ah, Mother, you are going to be dreary—I can feel it in my bones. And after we have been such good pals, too. I never would have believed it of you—of all people!"

"But, son, you can't go against convention like this!"

"All right, Mother, let us have it right out in the open like civilized persons. Exactly and precisely, what possible objection could you or anyone else have to Myron and me becoming husband and husband?"

"You know perfectly well why I object—he is Jewish!"

People are so much against each other. They have been conditioned for this antagonism for so long that they have forgotten completely that we are all human beings, that we belong to the same earth, to the same planet.

The greater the distance between the wife and the husband, the better will be the by-product of the marriage. And the same happens in music, in painting, in mathematics, in physics, in chemistry—a kind of crossbreeding. Whenever a person moves from one discipline to another discipline he brings the flavor of his discipline, although that discipline cannot be practiced. What can you do with your music when you go into physics? You have to forget all about it, but it remains in the background. It has become part of you; it is going to affect whatsoever you do. Physics is so far away, but if you have been disciplined in music, sooner or later you will find theories, hypotheses, which somehow have the color and the fragrance of music. You may start feeling that the world is a harmony—not a chaos but a cosmos. You may start feeling, searching into deeper realms of physics, that existence is an orchestra. Now, that is not possible for one who has not known anything of music.

If a dancer moves into music he will bring something new, he will contribute something new to music.

My suggestion is that people should go on moving from one discipline into another discipline. When you become accustomed to one discipline, when you become imprisoned with the technique, just slip out of it into another discipline. It is a good idea, a great idea to go on moving from one discipline into another. You will find yourself becoming more and more creative.

One thing has to be remembered: if you are really creative you may not become famous. A really creative person takes time to become famous because he has to create the values—new values, new criteria, only then can he be judged. He has to wait at least fifty years; by that time he is dead. Only then people start appreciating him. If you want fame, then forget all about creativity. Then just practice and practice, and just go on doing the thing that you are doing more skillfully, more technically perfectly, and you will be famous—because people understand it; it is already accepted.

Whenever you bring something new into the world you are bound to be rejected. The world never forgives a person who brings anything new to the world. The creative person is bound to be punished by the world, remember it. The world appreciates the uncreative but skillful person, the technically perfect person, because technical perfection simply means perfection of the past. And everybody understands the past, everybody has been educated to understand it. To bring something new into the world means nobody will be able to appreciate it; it is so new that there are not any criteria against which it can be valued. No means are yet in existence that can help people to understand it. It will take at least fifty years or more—the artist will be dead—by that time people will start appreciating it.

Vincent Van Gogh was not appreciated in his day. Not even a single painting was ever sold. Now each of his paintings is sold for millions of dollars—and people were not ready even to accept those paintings as gifts from Vincent Van Gogh—the same paintings! He had given them to friends, to anybody who was ready to hang them in their room. Nobody was ready to hang his pictures in their rooms because people were worried others would ask, "Have you gone mad or something? What kind of painting is this?"

Vincent Van Gogh had his own world. He has brought a new vision. It took many decades; slowly, humanity started feeling that something was there. Humanity is slow and lethargic, it lags behind time. And the creative person is always ahead of his time, hence the gap.

So if you really want to be creative you will have to accept that you can't be famous, you can't be well known. If you really want to be creative, then you have to learn the simple phenomenon of "art for art's sake," for no other motive. Then enjoy whatsoever you are doing. If you can find a few friends to enjoy it,

> Everybody understands the past, everybody has been educated to understand it. To bring something new into the world means nobody will be able to appreciate it; it is so new that there are not any criteria against which it can be valued.

good; if nobody is there to enjoy, then enjoy it alone. If *you* are enjoying it, that is enough. If you feel fulfilled through it, that is enough.

You ask me, "I am not sure anymore what the qualities of true art are."

True art means if it helps you to become silent, still, joyous; if it gives you a celebration, if it makes you dance—whether anybody participates with you or not is irrelevant. If it becomes a bridge between you and God, that is true art. If it becomes a meditation, that is true art. If you become absorbed in it, so utterly absorbed that the ego disappears, that is true art.

So don't be worried what true art is. If you rejoice in doing it, if you feel lost in doing it, if you feel overwhelmed with joy and peace in doing it, it is true art. And don't be bothered what critics say. Critics don't know anything about art. In fact, the people who cannot become artists become critics. If you cannot participate in a running race, if you cannot be an Olympic runner, at least you can stand by the side of the road and throw stones at other runners; that you can do easily.

That's what critics go on doing. They can't be participants, they can't create anything.

I have heard about a Sufi mystic who loved painting, and all the critics of his time were against him. Everybody would come and show him, "This is wrong, that is wrong."

He became tired of these people, so one day, in front of his house he hung all his paintings. And he invited all the critics and told them to come with brushes, with colors, so that they can correct his paintings—they have criticized enough; now the time has come to correct.

Not a single critic turned up. It is easy to criticize, it is difficult to correct. And after that, critics stopped criticizing his paintings. He did the right thing!

> Enjoy whatsoever you are doing. If you can find a few friends to enjoy it, good, if nobody is there to enjoy, then enjoy it alone. If *you* are enjoying it, that is enough. If you feel fulfilled through it, that is enough.

People who don't know how to create become critics—so don't be worried about them. The decisive thing is your inner feeling, inner glow, inner warmth. If making music gives you a feeling of warmth, joy arises in you, ego disappears, then it becomes a bridge between you and God. Art can be the most prayerful thing, the most meditative thing possible. If you can be in any art, music, painting, sculpture, dance, if any art can take a grip on your being, that's the best way to pray, the best way to meditate. Then you don't need any other meditation; that is your meditation. That will lead you slowly slowly, step by step, into God. So this is my criterion: if it leads you toward God, it is true art, it is authentic art.

4. THE ART OF MONEY

Can you talk about money? What are all these feelings that are around money? What makes it so powerful that people sacrifice their lives for it?

This is a very significant question.

All the religions have been against wealth because wealth can give you all that can be purchased in life. And almost everything can be purchased except those spiritual values like love, compassion, enlightenment, freedom. These few things are exceptions—and exceptions always prove the rule. Everything else you can purchase with money. Because all the religions have been against life, they were bound to be against money. That is a natural corollary. Life needs money because life needs comforts, life needs good food, life needs good clothes, good houses. Life needs beautiful literature, music, art, poetry. Life is vast!

And a man who cannot understand classical music is poor. He is deaf. He may hear—his eyes, his ears, his nose, all his senses will be perfectly right medically—but metaphysically . . . Can you see the beauty of great literature, like *The Book of Mirdad*? If you cannot see it, you are blind.

I have come across people who have not even heard of *The Book of Mirdad*. If I am to make a list of the great books, that will be the first. But to see the beauty of it you will need a tremendous discipline.

To understand classical music is possible only if you learn— and it is a long learning. To learn, you will need to be free from hunger, free from poverty, free from all kinds of prejudices.

For example, Mohammedans have prohibited music; now they have deprived man of a tremendous experience. It happened in New Delhi . . . one of the most powerful Mohammedan emperors, Aurangzeb, was on the throne. And he was not only powerful, he was really terrible.

Up to his time Mohammedan emperors were saying only that music was against Islam, but that was all; Delhi was full of musicians. But Aurangzeb was not a gentleman. He declared that if any music was heard in Delhi, the musician would be immediately beheaded. And Delhi was the center, naturally, because it was the capital for thousands of years. So it was the place where all kinds of geniuses were living.

When this declaration was made, all the musicians gathered together and they said, "Something has to be done, this is too much! They used to say it is against Islam—that was okay. But this man is dangerous, he will start killing." So as a protest, all the musicians— of which there were thousands—went to Aurangzeb's palace.

He came on the balcony and asked the people, "Who has

died?"—because what they had done . . . they were carrying a corpse the way it is carried in India. There was no corpse inside, just pillows, but they had managed to make it look like a corpse. Aurangzeb asked, "Who has died?"

And they answered, "Music. And you are the murderer of it."

Aurangzeb said, "Good that it has died. Now please be kind enough to me—dig as deep a grave as possible, so that it can never come out from the grave again." Those thousands of musicians and their tears had no effect on Aurangzeb—he was doing something "sacred."

Music is denied by Mohammedans. Why? Because music was basically played in the East by beautiful women. In the East and in the West the meaning of the word *prostitute* differs. In the West the prostitute is selling her body. In the East, in the past, the prostitute was not selling her body; she was selling her genius, her dance, her music, her art.

You will be surprised that every Indian king used to send his sons, who were going to become his successors, to live with great prostitutes for a few years. They were sent to learn etiquette, to learn gentleness, to learn music, to learn the delicacies of dance— because a king should be really rich about everything. He should understand beauty, he should understand logic, he should understand manners. That has been the old Indian tradition.

Mohammedans disrupted it. Music was against their religion. Why? Because to learn music you had to enter a prostitute's house. Mohammedans are very much against any rejoicing, and the house of the prostitute was full of laughter, songs, music, dance. They simply prohibited it: no Mohammedan could enter a place of music; to hear music was a sin.

And the same has been done by different religions—for different reasons, but they have all been cutting man's richness. And the most basic teaching is that you should renounce money.

You can see the logic. If you don't have money, you can't have anything else. Rather than cutting branches, they were cutting the very roots. A man without money is hungry, is a beggar, has no clothes. You cannot expect him to have time for Dostoyevsky, Nijinsky, Bertrand Russell, Albert Einstein, no; that is impossible.

All the religions together have made man as poor as possible. They have condemned money so much, and praised poverty so much, that as far as I am concerned, they are the greatest criminals the world has known.

Look what Jesus says: A camel can pass through the eye of a needle, but a rich man cannot pass through the gates of heaven. Do you think this man is sane? He is ready to allow a camel to pass through the eye of a needle—which is absolutely impossible, but even that impossibility he accepts may be made possible. But a rich man entering into paradise? That is a far bigger impossibility; there is no way to make it possible.

Wealth is condemned, richness is condemned, money is condemned. The world is left in two camps. Ninety-eight percent of the people live in poverty but with a great consolation, that where rich people will not be able to enter, they will be received with angels playing on their harps, "Alleluia . . . Welcome!" And the two percent who are rich are living with tremendous guilt that they are rich.

They cannot enjoy their richness because of the guilt, and they are deep down afraid: perhaps they may not be allowed to enter into paradise. So they are in a dilemma. Riches are creating guilt in them—they will not be consoled because they are not mourning—they will not be allowed in paradise because they are having so many things on the earth. They will be thrown into hell.

Because of this situation, the rich man lives in a very fearful state. Even if he enjoys, or tries to enjoy things, his guilt poisons it. He may be making love to a beautiful woman, but it is only the body that is making love. He is thinking of paradise where camels are entering, and he is standing outside and there is no way to go in. Now can this man make love? He may be eating the best food possible, but he cannot enjoy it. He knows this life is short, and after that is just darkness and hellfire. He lives in paranoia.

The poor man is already living in hell, but he lives with a consolation. You will be surprised to know that in poor countries people are more contented than in rich countries. I have seen the poorest people in India with no dissatisfaction at all. And Americans are going around the world to find some spiritual guidance—naturally, because they don't want to be defeated by camels; they want to enter into the gates of heaven. They want to find some way, some yoga, some exercises, as a compensation.

This whole world has been turned against itself.

Perhaps I am the first person who is respectful of money, of wealth, because it can make you multidimensionally rich.

A poor man cannot understand Mozart, a hungry man cannot understand Michelangelo, a beggar will not even look at the paintings of Vincent Van Gogh. And people who are suffering from hunger don't have enough energy to make them intelligent. Intelligence comes only when you have superfluous energy in you—they are exhausted just in earning bread and butter. They don't have intelligence, they cannot understand *The Brothers Karamazov*, they can only listen to some stupid priest in a church.

Neither the priest understands what he is talking about, nor the audience. Most of them are fast asleep, tired after six days of work. And the priest finds it more comfortable that everybody is asleep, so he need not prepare a new sermon. He can go on using the old sermon. Everybody is asleep, nobody will figure out that he is just cheating them.

Wealth is as significant as beautiful music, as great literature, as masterpieces of art.

There are people who have a born capacity to be a musician. Mozart started playing beautiful music at the age of eight. When he was eight, other great masters of music were not anywhere near him. Now, this man is born with that creativity. Vincent Van Gogh was born of a poor father who worked in a coal mine. He never got educated, he never knew any art school, but he became one of the greatest painters of the world.

Just a few days ago I saw a picture of one of his paintings. For that painting he was laughed at by all painters, what to say about others?—because he had painted stars in a way nobody had seen stars: like nebulae, every star in movement, like a wheel turning continuously. Who had seen stars like that?

Even other painters said, "You are going mad—these are not stars!" And moreover, the trees that he painted underneath the stars are going higher than the stars. Stars are left far behind, trees have reached far ahead. Now who has seen such trees? This is just madness!

But a few days ago I saw a picture of this type. Physicists have now discovered that Van Gogh is right: stars are not as they look, they are exactly the way Van Gogh has painted them. Poor Van Gogh! What eyes that man must have had, to see what physicists took one hundred years to find out, with all their big labs and big technology. And Vincent Van Gogh, strangely enough, just with bare eyes figured out the exact shape of the stars. They are whirling, they are whirling dervishes; they are not static the way you see them.

And when he was asked about his trees: "Where have you

found these trees, which go above the stars?" He said, "These are the trees I have found, sitting by their side listening to their ambitions. I have heard the trees say to me that they are the ambitions of the earth to reach to the stars."

Perhaps a few more centuries may be needed for scientists to discover that certainly the trees are the ambitions of the earth. One thing is certain, that trees are moving against gravitation. The earth is allowing them to move against gravitation—supporting, helping them. Perhaps the earth wants some communication with the stars. The earth is alive, and life always wants to go higher and higher and higher. There is no limit to its aspirations. How are the poor people going to understand? They don't have the intelligence.

Just as there are born poets, born painters, I would like you to remember there are born wealth creators. They have never been appreciated. Everybody is not a Henry Ford, and cannot be.

Henry Ford was born poor and became the richest man in the world. He must have had some talent, some genius for creating money, for creating wealth. And that is far more difficult than to create a painting, or music, or poetry. To create wealth is not an easy job. Henry Ford should be praised just as any master musician, novelist, poet— in fact, he should be praised more, because with his money all the poetry and all the music and all the sculptures of the world can be purchased.

I respect money. Money is one of the greatest inventions of man. It is just a means. Only idiots have been

> Just as there are born poets, born painters, I would like you to remember there are born wealth-creators. They have never been appreciated.

> ☙
>
> To create wealth is not an easy job. Henry Ford should be praised just as any master musician, novelist, poet—in fact, he should be praised more, because with his money all the poetry and all the music and all the sculptures of the world can be purchased.

condemning it; perhaps they were jealous that others have money and they don't. Their jealousy became their condemnation.

Money is nothing but a scientific way of exchanging things. Before there was money, people were in real difficulty. All over the world there was a barter system. You have a cow and you want to purchase a horse. Now it is going to be your whole lifelong task. . . . You have to find a man who wants to sell a horse and wants to purchase a cow. It is so difficult a job! You may find people who have horses but they are not interested in buying cows. You may find people who are interested in buying cows but they don't have horses.

That was the situation before money came into existence. Naturally, people were bound to be poor: they could not sell things, they could not buy things. It was such a difficult job. Money made it so simple. The man who wants to sell the cow need not search for the man who wants to sell his horse. He can simply sell the cow, take the money, and find the man who wants to sell the horse but is not interested in a cow.

Money became the medium of exchange; the barter system disappeared from the world. Money did a great service to humanity—and because people became capable of purchasing, selling, naturally they became more and more rich.

This has to be understood. The more money moves, the more money you have. For example, if I have one dollar with me. . . . It is just for example, I don't have one, I don't have even a cent with me—I don't even have pockets! Sometimes I get worried that if I get a dollar, where am I going to keep it? For example, if I have a dollar and I go on keeping it to myself, then in this auditorium there is only one dollar. But if I purchase something and the dollar moves to somebody else, I get the worth of the dollar, which I will enjoy. You cannot eat the dollar, how can you enjoy it just by keeping it? You can enjoy it only by spending it. I enjoy, and the dollar reaches somebody else. Now if he keeps it, then there are only two dollars—one I have enjoyed already, and one is with that miser who is keeping it.

But if nobody is a clinger, and everybody is moving the dollar as fast as possible—if there are three thousand people, three thousand dollars have been used, enjoyed. That is one single round. Just give more rounds and there will be more dollars. Nothing is coming in—there is, in fact, only one dollar—but by moving it goes on multiplying itself.

That's why money is called currency—it should be a current. That's my meaning, I don't know about others' meanings. One should not keep it. The moment you get it,

> ☙
>
> Money is a tremendous invention. It makes people richer, it makes people capable of having things that they don't have. But all the religions have been against it.

> ❧
>
> Drop all ideas that have been imposed upon you about money. Be respectful to it. Create wealth, because only after creating wealth do many other dimensions open for you.

spend it! Don't waste time, because that much time you are preventing the dollar from growing, from becoming more and more.

Money is a tremendous invention. It makes people richer, it makes people capable of having things that they don't have. But all the religions have been against it. They don't want humanity to be rich and they don't want humanity to be intelligent, because if people are intelligent, who is going to read the Bible?

Religions never wanted man to be intelligent, never wanted man to be rich, never wanted man to rejoice, because people who are in suffering, poor, unintelligent—they are the clients of churches, synagogues, temples, mosques.

I have never gone to any religious place. Why should I go? If the religious place wants to have some taste of religion it should come to me. I am not going to Mecca, Mecca has to come to me! I am not going to Jerusalem, I am not mad—just a little bit crazy, but not mad. And when we can create a place of joy and laughter and love here, what is there in Israel? We have created the new Israel.

Drop all ideas that have been imposed upon you about money. Be respectful to it. Create wealth, because only after creating wealth do many other dimensions open for you.

CREATION

The Ultimate Creativity, The Meaning of Your Life

Life in itself has no meaning. Life is an opportunity to create meaning. Meaning has not to be discovered: it has to be created. You will find meaning only if you create it. It is not lying there somewhere behind the bushes, so you can go and you search a little bit and find it. It is not there like a rock that you will find. It is a poetry to be composed, it is a song to be sung, it is a dance to be danced.

Meaning is a dance, not a rock. Meaning is music. You will find it only if you create it. Remember it.

Millions of people are living meaningless lives because of this utterly stupid idea that meaning has to be discovered. As if it is already there. All that you need is to just pull the curtain, and behold! meaning is here. It is not like that.

So remember, Buddha finds the meaning because he creates it. I found it because I created it. God is not a thing but a creation. And only those who create find. And it is good that meaning is not lying there somewhere, otherwise one person would have discovered it— then what would be the need for everybody else to discover it?

Can't you see the difference between religious meaning and

> Millions of people are living meaningless lives because of this utterly stupid idea that meaning has to be discovered. As if it is already there, all that you need is to just pull the curtain, and behold! meaning is there. It is not like that.

scientific meaning? Albert Einstein discovered the theory of relativity; now, do you have to discover it again and again? You will be foolish if you discover it again and again. What is the point? One man has done it; he has given you the map. It may have taken years for him, but for you to understand it will take hours. You can go to the university and learn.

Buddha also discovered something, Zarathustra also discovered something, but it is not like Albert Einstein's discovery. It is not there such that you have just to follow Zarathustra and his map and you will find it—you will never find it. You will have to become a Zarathustra. See the difference!

To understand the theory of relativity, you need not become an Albert Einstein, no. You have to be just of average intelligence, that's all. If you are not too much retarded, you will understand it.

But to understand the meaning of Zarathustra, you will have to become a Zarathustra—less than that won't do. You will have to create it again. And each individual has to give birth to God, to meaning, to truth; each man has to become pregnant with it and pass through the pains of birth. Each one has to carry it in one's womb, feed it by one's own blood, and only then does one discover.

If you can't see any meaning in life, you must be waiting passively for the meaning to come . . . it will never come. This has been the idea of the past religions, that the meaning is already there. It is not! Freedom is there to create it, energy is there to create it. The field is there to sow the seeds and reap the crop. All is there— but the meaning has to be created. That's why to create it is such a joy, such an adventure, such an ecstasy.

So the first thing: religion has to be creative. Up to now, religion has remained very passive, almost impotent. You don't expect a religious person to be creative. You just expect him to fast, sit in a cave, get up early in the morning, chant mantras . . . and this kind of stupid thing. And you are perfectly satisfied! What is he doing? And you praise him because he goes on long fasts. Maybe he is a masochist, maybe he enjoys torturing himself. He sits there when it is icy cold, naked, and you appreciate him.

But what is the point, what is the value in it? All the animals of the world are naked in the icy cold— they are not saints. Or when it is hot, he sits in the hot sun, and you appreciate him. You say, "Look! here is a great ascetic." But what is he doing? What is his contribution to the world? What beauty has he added to the world? Has he changed the world a little bit? Has he made it a little more sweet, more fragrant? No, you don't ask that.

Now, I tell you, this has to be

> Life is not there readymade, available. You get the life that you create, you get out of life that which you put into it. First you have to pour meaning into it. You have to give color and music and poetry, you have to be creative. Only then will you be alive.

asked. Praise a man because he has created a song. Praise a man because he has created a beautiful sculpture. Praise a man because he plays such a beautiful flute. Let these be religious qualities from now onward. Praise a man because he is such a lover—love is religion. Praise a man because through him, the world is becoming more graceful.

Forget all these stupid things like fasting and just sitting in a cave, torturing oneself, or lying down on a bed of nails. Praise a man because he has cultivated beautiful roses; the world is more colorful because of him. And then you will find meaning. Meaning comes out of creativity. Religion has to become more poetic, more aesthetic.

> Praise a man because he has created a beautiful sculpture. Praise a man because he plays such a beautiful flute. Let these be religious qualities from now on.

And second thing: sometimes it happens that you search for the meaning because you have already concluded. Out of a conclusion you search for it—you have already decided what meaning should be there, or must be there—and then you don't find it.

The inquiry has to be pure. What do I mean when I say the inquiry has to be pure? It should be without any conclusion. It should not have any a priori in it. What meaning are you looking for? If you have already concluded that you are looking for a certain meaning, you will not find it—because from the very beginning your inquiry is polluted, your inquiry is impure. You have already decided.

For example, if a man comes into my garden and thinks if he can find a diamond there, only then this garden is beautiful . . . And he cannot find the diamond, so he says there is no meaning in the garden. There are so many beautiful flowers and so many birds singing, and so many colors, and the wind blowing through the pines, and the moss on the rocks. But he cannot see any meaning because he has a certain idea—he has to find the diamond, a Kohinoor, only then will there be meaning. He is missing meaning because of his idea.

Let your inquiry be pure. Don't move with any fixed idea; go naked and nude. Go open and empty. And you will find not only one meaning, you will find a thousand and one meanings. Then each thing will become meaningful. Just a colored stone shining in the rays of the sun . . . or a dewdrop creating a small rainbow around itself . . . or just a small flower dancing in the wind. . . . What meaning are you searching for?

Don't start with a conclusion, otherwise you have started wrongly from the very beginning. Go without a conclusion! That's what I mean when I say again and again, go without knowledge if you want to find truth. The knowledgeable person never finds it, his knowledge is a barrier.

Goldstein had never been to a show in the legitimate theater. For his birthday, his children decided to give him a present of a ticket.

The night after the show, they came to visit him and asked him eagerly what he thought of it. "Ach," he answered, "it was simply nonsense. When she was willing, he wasn't willing. And when he was willing, she wasn't willing. And when they both were willing, down came the curtain!"

> ❧
>
> Don't move with any fixed idea. Go naked and nude. Go open and empty. And you will find not only one meaning, you will find a thousand and one meanings.

Now, if you have a fixed idea, then you are only looking for it, only looking for it. . . . And because of this narrowness of the mind, all that is available is missed. Meaning has to be created. And meaning has to be searched for without any conclusions. If you can drop your knowledge, life will suddenly take on color—it will become psychedelic. But you are continuously carrying the load of your scriptures, books, theories, doctrines, philosophies . . . you are lost in all that. And everything has become mixed up, hotchpotch, and you cannot even remember what is what.

Your mind is a mess. Clean it! Make it a blank. The empty mind is the best mind. And those who have been telling you that the empty mind is the devil's workshop are the devil's agents. The empty mind is closer to God than anything. The empty mind is not the devil's workshop. The devil cannot do without thoughts. With emptiness the devil cannot do anything at all. He has no way into emptiness.

So many thoughts in the mind, mixed up; nothing seems to be clear; you have heard so many things from so many sources—your mind is a monster! And you are trying to remember, and you have been told to remember: "Don't forget!" And, naturally, the burden is such that you cannot remember. Many things you have forgotten. Many things you have imagined and added on your own.

An Englishman visiting America attended a banquet and heard the master of ceremonies give the following toast: "Here's to the happiest moment of my life,
Spent in the arms of another man's wife—my mother."

"By Jove, that's ripping," the Englishman thought to himself. "I must remember to use it back home."

Some weeks later when he returned to England, he attended a church luncheon and was asked to give a toast. In thunderous tones he addressed the crowded room: "Here's to the happiest moment of my life,
Spent in the arms of another man's wife . . ."

After a long pause the crowd began to grow restless, glaring at the speaker indignantly. The speaker's friend sitting next to him whispered, "You had better explain yourself quickly."

"By Jove," the speaker blurted out, "you will have to excuse me. I forgot the name of the bloomin' woman."

That is happening. You remember this—"Plato has said this." And you remember that—"Lao Tzu has said that." And you remember what Jesus has said, and what Mohammed has said . . . and you remember many things, and they have all got mixed up, and you have not said a single thing on your own. Unless you say something on your own, you will miss the meaning.

Drop the knowledge and become more creative. Remember, knowledge is gathered—you need not be creative about it; you have only to be receptive. And that's what man has become: man is reduced to being a spectator. He reads the newspapers, he reads the Bible and the Koran and the Gita; he goes to the movie, sits

> ❧
>
> Meaning comes through participation. Participate in life! Participate as deeply, as totally, as possible. Risk all for participation. If you want to know what dance is, don't go and see a dancer—learn dancing, be a dancer. If you want to know anything, participate.

there and watches the movie; he goes to the football match, or sits before his TV, listens to the radio . . . and so on and so forth. Twenty-four hours a day he is just in a kind of inactivity, a spectator. Others are doing things and he is simply watching.

You will not find meaning by watching. You can see a thousand and one lovers making love and you will not know what love is—you will not know that orgasmic abandonment by watching. You will have to become a participant—meaning comes through participation. Participate in life! Participate as deeply, as totally, as possible. Risk all for participation. If you want to know what dance is, don't go and see a dancer—learn dancing, be a dancer. If you want to know anything, participate! That is the true and the right way, the authentic way, to know a thing. And there will be great meaning in your life—not only one-dimensional, multidimensional meanings. You will be showered by meanings.

Life has to be multidimensional, then only is there meaning. Never make life one-dimensional. That too is a problem. Somebody becomes an engineer, and then he thinks all is finished, he becomes identified with being an engineer. Then his whole life he is just an engineer . . . and there were millions of things available but he moves only on one track. He becomes bored, is fed up. Is tired, wearied. Goes on dragging. Waits only for death. What meaning can there be?

Have more interests in life. Don't be always a businessman; sometimes play too. Don't be just a doctor or an engineer, or a headmaster, or a professor—be as many things as possible! Play cards, play the violin, sing a song, be an amateur photographer, a poet. . . . Find as many things as possible in life, and then you will have richness. And meaning is a by-product of richness.

I have heard a very meaningful story about Socrates:

Socrates, while awaiting death in prison, was haunted by a dream that kept urging him, "Socrates, make music!" The old man felt he had always served art with his philos-ophizing. But now, spurred on by that mysterious voice, he turned fables into verse, composed a hymn to Apollo, and played the flute.

In the face of death, philosophy and music briefly went hand in hand, and Socrates was as blissful as never before.

He had never played on the flute. Something inside him per-sisted, "Socrates, make music!" Just in the face of death! It looked so ridiculous. And he had never played, he had never made music. A part of his being had remained suffocated—yes, even a man like Socrates, had remained one-dimensional. The denied part insisted, "Enough of logic—a little music will be good, will bring balance. Enough of argumentation—play on the flute." And the voice was so persistent that he had to yield to it.

His disciples must have been puzzled: "Has he gone mad? Soc-rates playing on the flute?" But to me it is very significant. The music could not have been very great, because he had never played. Absolutely amateurish, childish it must have been—but still something was satisfied, something was bridged. He was no longer one-sided. For the first time in his life, maybe, he was spontaneous. For the first time he had done something for which he could not supply any reason. Otherwise, he was a rational man.

Just the other night I was reading a story about the great Hasidic mystic Baal Shem:

It was a holiday, and the Hasidim had gathered to pray and to have a communion—*satsang*—with the master. A man had come with his retarded child. He was a little worried about the boy, he might do something, so he was keeping an eye on him. When the prayers were said, the boy asked his father, "I have got a whistle—can I play on it?"

The father said, "Absolutely no—where is your whistle?" because he was afraid, the boy may not even listen to his no. He showed the father where the whistle was, in his pocket, and the father kept his eye on that pocket, on the boy. Then there was dancing, and the father forgot and he also started dancing. The Hasidim were dancers, joyous people—the cream of Judaism, the very essence of Judaism was with them, with those mad people.

When everybody was praying to God and dancing, suddenly

> Let there be moments, unexplainable. Let there be a few things that are mysterious, for which you cannot supply any reason. Let there be a few doings for which people will think you are a little crazy.

the boy could not resist anymore. He took out his whistle and blew on it. Everybody was shocked! But Baal Shem came, hugged the boy, and said, "Our prayers are heard. Without this whistle, all was futile—because this was the only spontaneous thing here. All else was ritual."

Don't allow your life to become just a dead ritual. Let there be moments, unexplainable. Let there be a few things that are mysterious, for which you cannot supply any reason. Let there be a few doings for which people will think you are a little crazy. A man who is a hundred percent sane is dead. A little bit of craziness by the side is always a great joy. Go on doing a few crazy things, too. And then meaning will be possible.

About the Author

Osho is a contemporary mystic whose life and teachings have influenced millions of people of all ages and from all walks of life. He has been described by the *Sunday Times* in London as one of the "1000 Makers of the 20th Century" and by *Sunday Mid-Day* (India) as one of the ten people—along with Gandhi, Nehru, and Buddha—who have changed the destiny of India.

About his own work Osho has said that he is helping to create the conditions for the birth of a new kind of human being. He has often characterized this new human being as "Zorba the Buddha"—capable of enjoying both the earthy pleasures of a Zorba the Greek and the silent serenity of a Gautama the Buddha. Running like a thread through all aspects of Osho's work is a vision that encompasses both the timeless wisdom of the East and the highest potential of Western science and technology.

He is also known for his revolutionary contribution to the science of inner transformation, with an approach to meditation that acknowledges the accelerated pace of contemporary life. His unique "Active Meditations" are designed to first release the accumulated stresses of body and mind, so that it is easier to experience the thought-free and relaxed state of meditation.

Meditation Resort

Osho Commune International

Osho Commune International, the meditation resort that Osho established in India as an oasis where his teachings could be put into practice, continues to attract thousands of visitors per year from more than one hundred different countries around the world. Located about one hundred miles southeast of Bombay in Pune, India, the facilities cover thirty-two acres in a tree-lined suburb known as Koregaon Park. Although the resort itself does not provide accommodation for guests, there is a plentiful variety of nearby hotels.

The resort meditation programs are based in Osho's vision of a qualitatively new kind of human being who is able both to participate joyously in everyday life and to relax into silence. Most programs take place in modern, air-conditioned facilities and include everything from short to extended meditation courses, creative arts, holistic health treatments, personal growth, and the "Zen" approach to sports and recreation. Programs are offered throughout the year, alongside a full daily schedule of Osho's active meditations.

Outdoor cafes and restaurants within the resort grounds serve both traditional Indian fare and a variety of international dishes, all made with organically grown vegetables from the commune's own farm. The campus has its own private supply of safe, filtered water.

For booking information call (323) 563-6075 in the USA or check osho.com for the Pune Information Center nearest you.

For more information: www.osho.com

A comprehensive Web site in different languages, featuring an on-line tour of the meditation resort, information about books and tapes, Osho information centers worldwide, and selections from Osho's talks.

Osho International
570 Lexington Avenue
New York, NY 10022
Telephone: (212) 588-9888
Fax: (212) 588-1977
email: osho-int@osho.org.

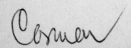